The Knowledge

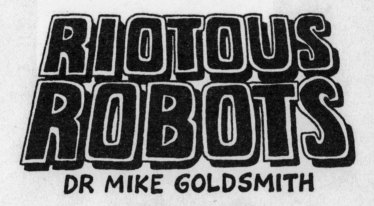

RIOTOUS ROBOTS

DR MIKE GOLDSMITH

Illustrated by
Mike Phillips

Hippo

With thanks to top roboticists Rod Brooks,
Murray Shanahan, Mark Tilden and
Kevin Warwick

Com

Scholastic Children's Books,
Commonwealth House, 1–19 New Oxford Street,
London WC1A 1NU, UK

A division of Scholastic Ltd
London ~ New York ~ Toronto ~ Sydney ~ Auckland
Mexico City ~ New Delhi ~ Hong Kong

Published in the UK by Scholastic Ltd, 2003

CONTENTS

INTRODUCTION

Everyone knows what robots are like. They're like this:

Or even as scary as this:

... aren't they? Well, we've all seen the films where robots are massacring every human in sight or taking over the world, but real robots are nothing like as scary. Though they can be a bit dangerous to hang around with while they're working, they're certainly not likely to kill us all – well, not yet anyway.

Films and stories make us think that robots are riotous but the reality is very different. Although a lot of robot scientists around today are strongly influenced by fictional robots (which we'll be meeting in the next chapter), the robots they build aren't quite the same. For one thing, fictional robots are able to act like people and can have a go at anything from dressmaking to falling in love, while real robots are normally designed to do just one sort of thing, like building cars or exploring Mars. That's why most real robots don't look like humans – our bodies have evolved to do absolutely loads of things fairly well, while robot bodies are designed to do a few things very well. Real robots are incredibly complicated machines that are far better at their jobs than people are and in this book you'll discover a whole host of them. We'll be meeting robots that can:

- feed on slugs using a three-fingered hand equipped with a slime scraper

- change shape using jets of quick-setting plastic

- crawl around inside you carrying spikes and knives
- use electric sandwiches to handle delicate things.

Read on and decide for yourself if humans are still in control of robots like these, or if our metal friends are about to take over the world...

REAL ROBOTS

So where did the idea that robots are dangerous come from? Well, it's all the fault of...

Scary stories

There have been legends of man-made monsters since at least the 16th century, and in 1818 Mary Shelley wrote the most famous man-made-monster story of all: *Frankenstein*. The monster is made out of bits and pieces from graveyards and is quite matey to begin with – until it discovers that its somewhat terrifying appearance puts people off it a bit, at which point it starts to kill them.

Frankenstein's creation was nameless, and it wasn't until the 20th century that robots got their name. In 1920, a Czechoslovakian writer called Karel Capek wrote a play called *Rossum's Universal Robots*, about some intelligent man-made creatures that conquered the world. The word "robot" means something like "low-grade worker" in Czech, and the ones in the play were just fine at first, working away efficiently at their boring low-grade jobs while the humans had all the fun. Unfortunately, one of the characters in the play gave them feelings, at which point they went a bit bananas and started killing people. In fact, they slaughtered just about everyone, including the people who knew how to build more robots, which was a bit careless of them.

Then, in the 1940s, a writer called Isaac Asimov started to write lots of short stories about humanoid (that is, human-shaped) robots. To make his robots more realistic, and to avoid too much mayhem and gore in the stories, he came up with a set of rules for them. His fictional robot-scientists built the rules into their robots to control them. Asimov called these rules the Laws of Robotics (a word he invented) and he first wrote them down in 1942 in a story called *Runaround*. They say that robots must:

① Not hurt people.

② Obey all instructions (unless that would mean hurting people).

③ Look after themselves (unless that would mean disobeying an instruction or hurting people).

Real roboticists (as robot-scientists are called) accept that these rules will need to be built into advanced robots before they're allowed to interact with humans.

There are lots of arguments about this, and nearly as many definitions as there are books about robotics, but most roboticists would go along with a definition like this:

Robot
A machine that can do a range of tasks in a human-like way.

The trouble is, other, simpler machines are sometimes referred to as robots. But never mind, things like that can still be in this book even if they're not what everyone would call a robot.

A what's what of robotic creatures

There are lots of types of robots and robot-like things lurching about and some are still just ideas. You'll need to know about them before you launch into this book, so here's a list of the main types:

1. Automata

Automata are machines, often clockwork, which are designed to look and move like living things. They've been around for thousands of years, and they have almost none of the flexibility of a modern robot – they are built to perform a very small number of tasks (like pouring wine and bowing) over and over again in exactly the same way, and though some seem intelligent, they aren't really.

WHAT A DUMB WAITER!

CLICK! CLICK! CLICK!

Automata were the earliest type of robotic machine, but they were really just for fun, unlike modern robots, which usually have serious jobs to do.

2. Puppet robots

Puppet robots are remote-controlled machines which can't do anything for themselves – they're just brainless bodies that can move, a bit like zombies but without that annoying smell of rotting flesh. The robots in *Robot Wars* and other fighting-robot TV shows are puppet robots. These are radio-controlled, but some puppet robots are linked to their controllers by cables. Puppet robots are sometimes called master-slave manipulators or telechirics.

3. Telepresence robots (T-bots)

T-bots are an advanced sort of puppet robot*. Telepresence is a system in which the human operator can see out of a puppet robot's "eyes", and sometimes even hear what it hears and feel what it feels.

In future, telepresence systems could be so advanced that the operator will really feel as if they

*T-bots are occasionally referred to as avatars or golems.

ARE the robot – even though they might be thousands of kilometres apart. Telepresence will probably be the nearest humans will get to actually wandering around on dangerous planets like Venus or distant ones like Pluto.

Factoid

There are plans for a T-bot to go to the Moon within a few years to give humans the chance to tour the lunar surface without leaving Earth. It will start its tour at Tranquillity Base, the site of the first human Moon landing in 1969.

4. Hybrids

Hybrids are puppet robots sometimes, but are switched over to self-control at others.

Some new airborne spy robots are like this – they mostly fly about all by themselves keeping an eye on things, but if they come across something that they're not equipped to deal with – like a fire – a human takes over control instead.

5. Animatrons

Animatronic machines, or animatrons, are a cross between automata and puppet robots. They imitate animals and monsters, like the dinosaurs in *Jurassic Park*, or the moving, roaring, bad-smelling* dinosaurs that live in the Natural History Museum in London.

*Honest. Sniff them and see.

16

6. Cyborgs

Cyborgs are halfway between animals – or people – and robots. They're living things with lots of added robotic bits. Proper cyborgs don't yet exist, but Professor Kevin Warwick has already become a REAL robot scientist by turning himself into a very basic cyborg – he implanted an electronic device into himself which allows him to communicate with computers and open electronic doors when he approaches.

And people with advanced artificial limbs are primitive cyborgs too.

7. Androids

Originally, "android" meant a very advanced type of robot which wasn't made out of gears and electronics, but was grown chemically instead. The robots in *Rossum's Universal Robots* were androids, but in the real world these sorts of creatures don't exist yet. These days, the word is applied to any robot that seems human, even if it does have gears inside. There are already some research robots about which do look just like people, though none move about in a convincing way yet.

Handier than humans?

Robots were invented for two main reasons:

1. Because people enjoy inventing and playing with amazing gadgets.

2. So that humans could avoid doing boring and dangerous jobs.

So, robots are given jobs we don't fancy, like mowing the lawn or dealing with bombs. They're good at these sorts of things because they:

- don't get bored
- don't mind doing dangerous things
- make more precise movements than we do
- are stronger than we are
- never forget instructions
- have incredibly steady hands (useful if there's a bit of brain surgery to be done (see page 151))
- don't mind staying up all night (even when they're not partying (which they never are))
- always do what they're told (well, so far anyway...).

But, before we meet all these mechanical marvels, let's take a look at where they started...

RIOTOUS ROBOTS TIMELINE

Robots have been around for a surprisingly long time. Their ancestors were moving statues and steam-driven models which were invented by Ancient Greek engineers thousands of years ago. But one of the earliest machines that people today call a robot was invented by someone who's more famous as a painter than a scientist...

1499 Leonardo da Vinci frightens the King of France with an automatic lion that walks up to him and shows him some flowers. Leonardo also designed a robotic knight that could stand up and wave its arms about.

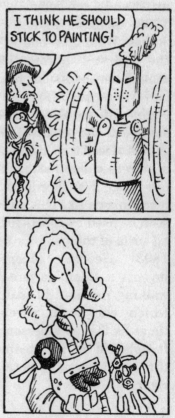

1730s French engineer Jacques de Vaucanson builds an automatic duck that can flap its wings, quack, eat and even go to the toilet, a flute-player that actually breathes, and a pipe-player that can play faster than any human. Each of the duck's wings contains over 400 moving parts.

1770s Swiss inventor Pierre Jaquet-Droz builds The Scribe. It sits at a desk, dips its quill pen in an inkwell and writes anything it's programmed to (so long as it doesn't take more than 40 letters). Jaquet-Droz also builds a mechanical artist and a musician.

1788 British inventor James Watt fits one of the first automatic control mechanisms, the Governor, to a steam engine. It regulates the speed of the engine so that it doesn't go BANG, a process called feedback (see page 53). Feedback mechanisms like this will soon be used by robots for all sorts of things.

1893 George Moore invents a steam-powered walking mechanical man which can walk three times as fast as a person. It gets rid of its steam through a handy metal cigar.

20

1906 A human-sized automaton is taken for a walk in London. It has staring eyes and its owner removes its head from time to time, to show it really *is* a robot. Traffic comes to a standstill, and the robot and its owner are arrested – a first in robot history.

1908 One of the first electrical machines to do household jobs automatically – the washing machine – is invented, an ancestor of the household robot.

1920 Robots get their name, and their reputation for being murderous monsters, in a play called *Rossum's Universal Robots*.

1926 An amazing fictional robot appears in *Metropolis*, a film set in a high-tech city of the future. The robot can change shape and is *thoroughly* wicked.

1930s Simple (but big and shiny) robots are popular at fairs. They do things like stand up, sit down, walk a step or two and smoke.

21

They're called names like Alpha, Elektro and Eric (which must have been an excitingly futuristic name in the 1930s). They're mostly humanoid and equipped with *extremely* shouty voices. Some of them are armed and dangerous. Elektro the Moto Man dances, counts to ten, smokes and boasts about all the other inventions made by its creator, the Westinghouse Electric company. It is accompanied by a little robotic dog called Sparko which can stand on its hind legs and bark.

1940s The very first electronic computers are constructed, big as buses and not much brighter. One called ENIAC weighed 30 tons and had the same processing power as a 6-mm-square microchip today! The first ancestors of hazard robots, remote-controlled arms called master-slave manipulators or Waldos, are used in the nuclear industry.

1942 Isaac Asimov comes up with some laws to make sure that robots don't wipe us all out.

1950s Lots of films and stories about robots appear, such as *Forbidden Planet*, *Zombies of the Stratosphere* and *The Day the Earth Stood Still*. Most of the robots are intelligent, humanoid and, despite Isaac Asimov, baaad!

1961 The first modern robot, UNIMATE, weighs in at 1,800 kg. Fortunately, it doesn't exterminate anyone, but settles for a nice repetitive factory job instead.

1963 Robots are popping up and killing people on every TV channel. The Daleks make their first appearance on British TV in *Dr Who*, turning it into the longest-running science-fiction TV series ever.

1964 One of the earliest robots that can move about is built. It is called The Beast, and it spends its time wandering around the corridors of John Hopkins

University in America, looking for prey. Luckily, it only eats electricity: when it finds a power socket it plugs itself in for a quick snack before wandering off again.

1966 The first successful single-purpose household robot is sold. It is called the Aqua Queen, and its descendants have been doing a great job cleaning private swimming pools ever since.

1968 A robot called Shakey (because it is) is built. It has primitive "eyes", a sense of touch, and can move about and push boxes around. (It can't pick them up because it hasn't got any arms, or enough brain-power to control them if it had). Shakey has two brains – it carries one with it and keeps in touch with the other by radio. It can't carry that brain too, because it's as big as a living-room.

1970s The microchip is developed, which means that computers are at last small enough to fit inside

robots. Robotic space probes explore the outer planets of the solar system.

1976 Two Viking robot probes land on the surface of Mars to look for Martians. Like Shakey, they have two brains each.

1977 *Star Wars* introduces famous friendly fictional robots R2D2 and C3P0.

1978 General-purpose factory robots called PUMAs (Programmable Universal Machine for Assembly) are produced by Unimation.

1980s Animatronic machines are built and used in films. There are lots of robots in factories, but the world recession causes a big decline in robot sales and puts more than 90% of robot companies out of business.

1990s The robot business recovers from its slump. Robots start to work successfully in teams, and some become artificially intelligent. Robotic planes and missiles are used in the

Gulf War, and a robot surgeon learns to operate on human brains.

1993 Rod Brooks starts to build Cog, an artificially intelligent robot that is designed to learn like a baby, by interacting with people and seeing and handling objects.

1996 P2 (which later became P3 and then Asimo), Honda's humanoid robot, is revealed after a decade of secret development. It is one of the most advanced – and expensive – robots ever and can climb stairs, open doors and shake hands like a person.

1997 A chess-playing machine called Deep Blue beats the world's best human chess player, and a robot called Sojourner explores the surface of Mars, making its own decisions as it moves about.

1999 The Aibo robot, a popular but pricey pet, goes on sale.

2002

- A robotic starfish that can turn somersaults is made in Japan. It is built from a jelly-like plastic which moves when an electric charge is applied to it.
- A new, more realistic-sounding robotic speech system is developed: instead of a loudspeaker it has artificial lungs, a plastic throat and rubber vocal cords.
- A dog-sized solar-powered robotic reporter is developed to interview people and film events in war zones and other dangerous places.

2003 The seventh robot soccer world cup is held.

FUN WITH ROBOTS

If you got a barking metal dog or a pig that can wiggle its snout for Christmas, congratulations. You're the proud owner of a descendant of the earliest robots – automata.

The automaton is the simplest type of robot, and very basic ones have been around for thousands of years. Automata don't react to what's going on around them, they just move through a set of actions, which means they aren't really very useful. They're fun though: in the 1490s, Leonardo da Vinci was designing and building impressive automata like the lion that could walk and, a bit like Bender in *Futurama*, open its chest to show what was inside (flowers, surprisingly enough).

More automata were built by craftsmen for rich customers over the next few centuries until, by the 18th century, every royal worth their crown had several in their court, playing instruments, dancing, and looking very stylish. Automata often wear very trendy clothes, unlike other types of robot, which are usually COMPLETELY NAKED (shocking, isn't it?).

Dolls that answer back

By the 19th century, simple clockwork automata could be bought even by non-rich people: for instance, fairly cheap baby-shaped crawling dolls were very popular in the 1870s. A non-walking robotic toy was invented by Thomas Edison, who's famous for inventing the light bulb even though he didn't (but that's another story). One of the many brilliant things he really did invent was the phonograph, which is the ancestor of the record player (which is the ancestor of the compact disc player). A phonograph contains a metal or wax cylinder with a needle resting on it. The needle is attached to a thin metal plate. As it rotates, a long groove on the cylinder makes the needle and plate wobble, and the wobbling of the plate can be heard as sounds. Famous inventors have to be at least as good at pushing their inventions as they are at inventing them in the first place, and in 1890 Edison launched a brilliant scheme to promote his phonographs. He put them inside dolls so the dolls could talk.

Edison's talking dolls were a great success and everyone wanted one for Christmas in the 1890s, just like everyone wanted a Buzz Lightyear 100 years later.

After that, there was no stopping robot toys, and dolls were soon walking, talking and going to sleep. It was all so exciting that some of them even wet themselves.

By the mid-20th century, clockwork robotic toys were being replaced by battery-powered ones. Meanwhile, the first computers were being built. They were far too big to be used in robots to start with, but in 1947, an electronic device called a transistor was invented, which made computers a lot smaller. Later on, the transistor was replaced by even

smaller components and computers shrank further until, towards the end of the century, they could be installed into some robot toys. This means today's toys can make all sorts of complicated movements and sounds. Often the movements are random, which is a very easy way of making a robot toy seem life-like, though it's the last thing you'd want any other type of robot to do!

Until recently, even the most advanced computerized toys have been either automata or puppet robots. But, at the end of the last century, the first of a new breed appeared:

A toy with a brain

The Sony Aibo robot dog went on sale in 1999. It's more than a toy – it's really a robotic pet. In fact, it's quite like a real dog who is a bit on the slow and metallic side, but which can take photos, dance and play with a ball. The latest versions of Aibos aren't modelled on dogs or cats, but something in between, and one thing that makes them very special is that they can learn to respond to human speech.

Name: Aibo
Function: robo-pet
Appearance: dogoid
Date (of first version): 1999
Weaknesses: non-fluffy, slower than a real dog
Robot-spotter's notes: Aibos are programmed to chase anything coloured bright pink

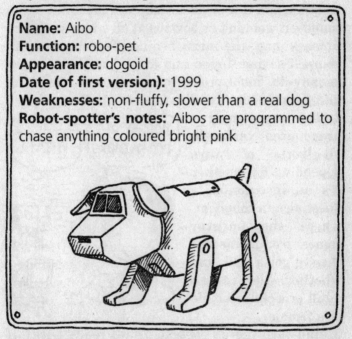

Listening machines

Any fictional robot worth its ray gun can react to human speech. It's very handy if real-life robots can do it too – it makes controlling a robot a lot easier if you can just tell it what you want. But it's not easy.

31

Automatic speech recognition

The basic idea of automatic speech recognition is simple: just record a whole set of sounds in a robot's memory, and program it to compare any words it hears with them, to see which is most similar. But this is much trickier than it sounds, for three reasons:

1. When we speak, we think that we say each word separately. But actually we don't – all the words run together, and if you saw a computer print-out of the sounds, it wouldn't be obvious at all where one word finishes and the next begins. Try listening to yourself saying "bread and butter" in the way you usually do. You'll probably actually say something like "brembudder", with no spaces at all.

2. The way a word is pronounced varies in all sorts of ways depending on whether it's an instruction, a question or a comment, where the speaker comes from, whether they've got a cold, and whether they're an adult or a child, a male or a female.

3. And then there's context. That's really tricky. If someone says "John had a little puppy", does that mean he had a small slice of one for breakfast? You can only decide if you understand the background information, or context – like whether John is a lion or a person.

It's easiest for a robot to cope with speech if it asks a human a question. If a person suddenly says "bill" to a robot, it won't know whether they're asking for a small piece of paper so they can pay for something, or describing a part of a small feathery animal. But if the robot has just asked the person for his name, it already knows what he's on about. If it's lucky.

Luckily it's easy enough for a robot to ask questions – making speech is a lot easier than recognizing it. Robots can do it very simply just by having a huge library of words, stringing them together and playing them through a loudspeaker. The only problem with this is that the speech comes out very flat and monotonous – which makes understanding them tricky. We're used to questions and exclamations sounding different to simple statements, so if a robot can't change its voice to make a question or exclamation sound the way we expect, it could have a few problems. For instance:

But it's quite easy to solve this problem, simply by making the pitch of the robot's voice change – making it rise at the end of a question for instance. Compared to speech recognition, making speech is easy. As those witty scientists say, "If making electronic speech is like squeezing toothpaste out of a tube, speech recognition is like putting it back in again." Which is why the first talking toy appeared over a century before the first listening one.

One way to make speech easier for robots to understand is to train the robot to recognize particular words spoken by a particular person, by getting the person to say the same set of words to it many times until it knows all the different ways the

34

person says them. This is what Aibos do, and it's called speaker-dependent speech recognition. The most advanced systems of this type can cope with over 50,000 different words.

So, being a toy or a pet is the sort of job which robots are really good at. But, it has to be said that, compared to other robots, these ones aren't terribly useful. In fact, you might say (if you're a heartless kind of person): A robot pet isn't for life. It's just for Christmas.

THE FACTORY FACTOR

Factory robots are by far the most common type of robot – there are over a million of them in use all over the world. Why? Because a lot of factory work involves obediently and accurately following the same set of instructions over and over again – something robots are very good at. And it costs a lot less to use a robot than pay a person, so robotic factories can produce things more cheaply than those employing humans (which is why manufactured goods are so cheap today). Also, humans just aren't much good at repetitive production-line-type jobs. They:

- get sleepy
- take decades
  to program properly
- forget things
- are easily damaged and
  expensive to repair
- get bored
- don't like working in
  dark, hot, cold, airless or
  noisy places
- need to be paid even
  after they've retired.

So, robots make ideal factory workers – no wonder they've been around longer than you have.

The machine age

The first factory robots appeared in the 1960s, but they weren't suddenly invented then. They were the final stage in the development of factory machines that started over a century before, which was all part of the industrial revolution. In the 1700s a sudden increase in the population of Britain meant there was a big demand for manufactured goods. There was also more money about, thanks to increased overseas trade. So lots of factories were built, full of new technology. Today's robots are largely the result of the industrial revolution, having evolved from simple single-task factory machines through more adaptable ones to the clever mechanisms we have today.

Weaving by numbers

One of the earliest ancestors of the factory robot was Jacquard's Loom, invented in 1801 by Monsieur Joseph Marie Jacquard. Normal looms are really fiddly and need a lot of attention, most of which is very repetitive. Now, repetition is what people hate but machines love. It makes them go all crackly with excitement. There were various automatic bits added to looms over the years, but it was Jacquard who did most to make the loom fully automatic. He invented a mechanical control system that would allow different patterns to be defined. All the user had to do to tell the loom what pattern to weave was to feed in some cards with holes punched in them. The holes directed threads of different colours into the right places, so by changing the cards you could change the pattern.

This made it different to all other looms but similar to a robot in that it could follow a set of pre-programmed instructions which could be easily modified.

A lathe with a brain

Seventy years after Jacquard built his loom, Mr Spence built another robot-ancestor. It was called the "Automat" lathe, and had two "brain wheels" which could be set in different ways so the lathe could do a range of things. It was a very narrow range: it could just make different sorts of grooves in things, but still it was a start. Spence and lots of others were very keen to develop robotic workers instead of employing people.

Down with robots!

But a lot of people really preferred *not* to be put out of work by machines, thanks very much, especially if the alternative was starving to death (as it was when the idea of replacing workers with machines began). So the automation of factories led to various riots and rebellions, and there is still some resistance to the idea. However, although it was a long time before the first factory robots appeared, factories continued to become more and more automated over the next few decades, and the importance of human factory workers declined.

The fear that factory robots might put people out of work led to a brilliant film: *Metropolis*. In an amazing city of the far future (well, 2026 actually), a whole army of robots is planned to replace human workers.

The humans work just like robots themselves, operating huge machines. (Actually, their jobs are so simple – pointing levers at light bulbs – that it would have been dead easy to build a really simple machine to replace them with anyway, without going to all the trouble of building an intelligent humanoid shape-shifting robot). The robot's design – and the basic idea of robots replacing humans whether they like it or not – has been copied in other films ever since.

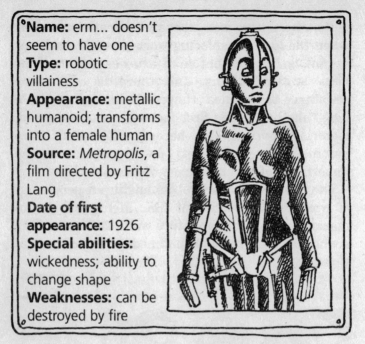

Name: erm... doesn't seem to have one
Type: robotic villainess
Appearance: metallic humanoid; transforms into a female human
Source: *Metropolis*, a film directed by Fritz Lang
Date of first appearance: 1926
Special abilities: wickedness; ability to change shape
Weaknesses: can be destroyed by fire

In the real world of the 1920s, nothing like the Metropolis robot was possible: factory machines, no matter how advanced, still needed a great deal of skilled human guidance. The first real factory robots started being developed in the early 1950s.

Mr Devol's amazing automatic scheme

The idea of a factory robot was developed by an American engineer called George Devol in the 1950s. At the time, factories were full of machines that were just great at making whatever it was they were designed to produce, whether it was plates or forks. But the machines were expensive and complicated to build, so it was only worth the money if the things they made could be sold in great quantities. If someone came up with a trendy new shape of plate or a clever six-pronged fork or something, the machines had to be more or less rebuilt to make them. But George had a great idea:

WHY NOT MAKE MACHINES THAT ARE DESIGNED TO DO LOTS OF THINGS INSTEAD OF JUST ONE THING?

So in 1954, George patented a programmable general-purpose machine that could move things from place to place in a factory – the first stage in the development of what he called a universal automatic machine. But he didn't actually build it – so far, it was just an idea.

It stayed that way until 1956, when George went to a cocktail party and met another engineer called Joe Engelberger.

SO I THOUGHT, WHY NOT MAKE AN ALL-PURPOSE FACTORY MACHINE.

YOU MEAN A ROBOT? GREAT IDEA, GEORGE. LET'S BUILD ONE...

Two years later, they did.

What George Devol and Joseph Engelberger came up with was, by today's standards, a very simple puppet robot, the Unimate. All it could do was pick things up and put them down again, but it was still very handy and successful. In 1961, Devol and Engelberger sold their first Unimate to the General Motors car plant in Trenton, New Jersey. There, it was set to work lifting and stacking pieces of hot metal – it went on working at the factory for over ten years. It didn't cause any riots – in fact, the workers really liked it since they didn't have to handle red-hot bits of car any more. Unimate wasn't controlled by a computer, but had an electronic system that meant it could be quickly instructed to move things about in whatever way was necessary, just as George Devol had suggested in his patent.

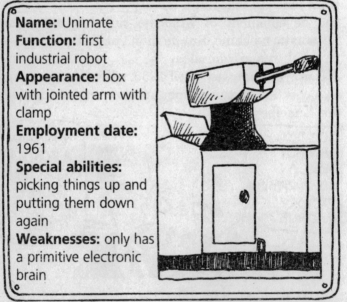

Name: Unimate
Function: first industrial robot
Appearance: box with jointed arm with clamp
Employment date: 1961
Special abilities: picking things up and putting them down again
Weaknesses: only has a primitive electronic brain

Joseph and George formed a company called Unimation, the first firm in the world to devote itself entirely to robotics. Sadly, Unimation's first profitable year wasn't until 1975 – it's not easy being first. But never mind – when Engelberger sold the company in 1983, he got $107 million for it!

Since Unimate, industrial robots have come a long way. There are thousands of factories operated mostly by robots, including most car factories, and soon there will be some with nothing but robots in them.

Factoid

In 1979, a Chrysler car plant in Detroit employed 200 welders to build car bodies. One year later, 50 robots had replaced the humans, and output had risen by 20%.

But today's factories aren't just *occupied* by robots and computers; they're designed by computers too, and the robots that go in them are often built by robots. In the next chapter, we'll find out how they work.

ROBOTS AT WORK

The commonest jobs for factory robots are:

- feeding components into machines
- collecting components from other machines
- welding
- spray-painting
- inserting electronic components into circuit boards
- soldering tiny wires in place.

Though there are thousands of different types of factory robot doing these jobs, they nearly all work in similar ways. One thing any self-respecting factory robot needs is some sort of arm and hand; in fact, a lot of them from Unimate onwards are not much more than that. There are now loads of arms (also called manipulators) to choose from, and each is best for one sort of job:

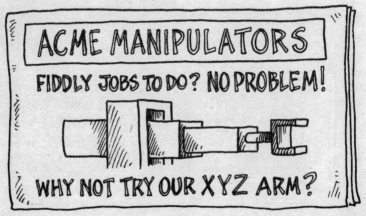

OR FOR YOU MUSCLE-BOTS OUT THERE WITH **BIG** LOADS...

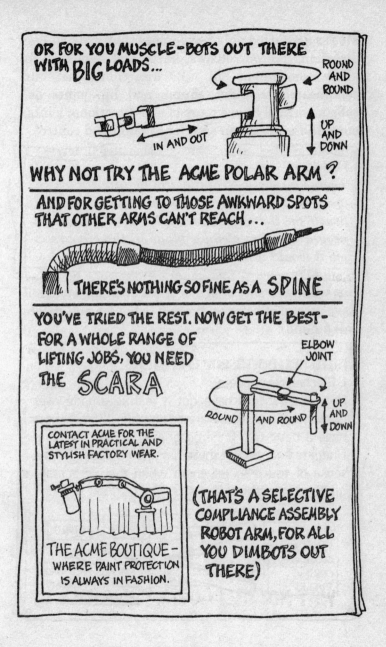

ROUND AND ROUND

IN AND OUT

UP AND DOWN

WHY NOT TRY THE ACME POLAR ARM?

AND FOR GETTING TO THOSE AWKWARD SPOTS THAT OTHER ARMS CAN'T REACH...

THERE'S NOTHING SO FINE AS A **SPINE**

YOU'VE TRIED THE REST. NOW GET THE BEST - FOR A WHOLE RANGE OF LIFTING JOBS, YOU NEED THE **SCARA**

ELBOW JOINT

ROUND AND ROUND

UP AND DOWN

CONTACT ACME FOR THE LATEST IN PRACTICAL AND STYLISH FACTORY WEAR.

THE ACME BOUTIQUE - WHERE PAINT PROTECTION IS ALWAYS IN FASHION.

(THAT'S A SELECTIVE COMPLIANCE ASSEMBLY ROBOT ARM, FOR ALL YOU DIMBOTS OUT THERE)

Most robot arms only have joints that work in one direction, like our elbows, knees and knuckles. To allow movement in all directions, as our complicated shoulder, thumb and hip joints do, robots normally have pairs of one-directional joints, since these are much simpler to build and control.

Factoid
There's a robotic cleaning arm for aircraft which is 26 m long, with eight joints and a rotating brush on the end. Though it takes a while to program, it can clean a plane in three hours: a job it would take a person 96 hours to do!

But whatever sort of arm a robot ends up with, it'll have an end effector on the end (what we non-robots call a hand).

NUTS AND BOLTS: END EFFECTORS
1. Mechanical grippers
Handwise, robots have got a real advantage over humans in that theirs are removable. Many robots have a basic two-fingered gripper, much like what Unimate had, except these days it's equipped with a sense of touch to tell them when they've actually grabbed something.

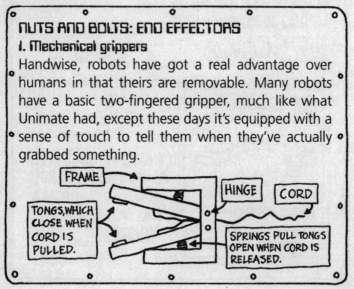

FRAME

HINGE

CORD

TONGS, WHICH CLOSE WHEN CORD IS PULLED.

SPRINGS PULL TONGS OPEN WHEN CORD IS RELEASED.

It's normally best to use compressed-air-powered ("pneumatic") hands, because the air, being compressible, gives the grip a nice bit of give. But to crush things, hydraulic power is best (see page 104).

2. Vacuum suckers

If a robot's job involves picking up nice smooth things like panes of glass, it can use a sucker that is vacuum controlled (these won't work in space though, since there's no air pressure to keep them stuck to things).

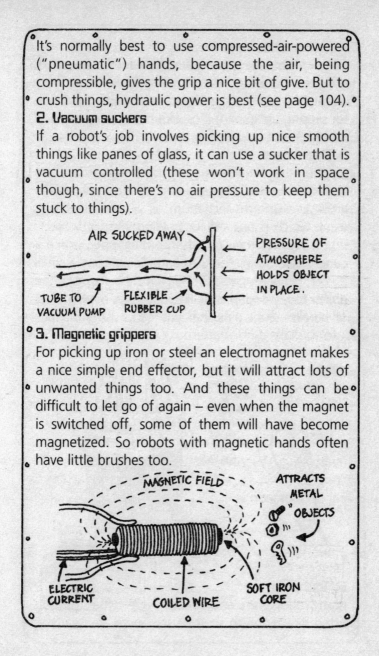

AIR SUCKED AWAY

PRESSURE OF ATMOSPHERE HOLDS OBJECT IN PLACE.

TUBE TO VACUUM PUMP

FLEXIBLE RUBBER CUP

3. Magnetic grippers

For picking up iron or steel an electromagnet makes a nice simple end effector, but it will attract lots of unwanted things too. And these things can be difficult to let go of again – even when the magnet is switched off, some of them will have become magnetized. So robots with magnetic hands often have little brushes too.

MAGNETIC FIELD

ATTRACTS METAL OBJECTS

ELECTRIC CURRENT

COILED WIRE

SOFT IRON CORE

4. Hooks and spikes

Some robots have very simple hands, like sticky grippers, hooks or even spikes. They're not very adaptable, but they're cheap and simple, and fine for picking up some things, like paper, suitcases and rubbish – but only in that order!

5. Superhands

On the other hand, some hands, though handy, are very complicated to make and control: one, called an Active Chord Mechanism, is like an elephant's trunk which is brilliant for holding irregular objects firmly, and another, called an omnigripper, is like a cube made of pins that can entirely surround a small object. Omnigrippers tell the robot the shape of the object too, working a bit like those toys made of lots of parallel blunt pins that you can push your face into to make a 3-D pattern.

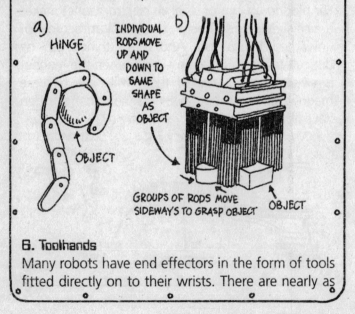

a) HINGE
OBJECT

INDIVIDUAL RODS MOVE UP AND DOWN TO SAME SHAPE AS OBJECT

b)

GROUPS OF RODS MOVE SIDEWAYS TO GRASP OBJECT   OBJECT

6. Toolhands

Many robots have end effectors in the form of tools fitted directly on to their wrists. There are nearly as many of these as there are jobs for robots to do: lasers, scalpels, drills, screwdrivers, clippers, paint-sprays... So that they can be changed easily, these effectors are usually fitted to the wrist with a bayonet fitting like that on a light bulb.

Factoid

The flexibot is a robotic hand and arm with a difference – it wanders around on its own, using its fingers to pull itself along and climb up things. The flexibot is still at the design stage, but the plan is to use it to help out in the home, fetching things, switching things on, and plugging things into the mains – including itself, when it's hungry.

Keeping track of limbs

We have a sense we hardly ever notice – the sense that tells us where our limbs are*. The only time

*This is called proprioreception.

49

we're likely to realize we
have this sense is when it
stops working – like when
you go to sleep on your arm
and wake up to see a scary
hand you don't recognize in
front of you. "Oh, no!" you
think. "And, just a minute,

where's *my* hand?" It's very important for a factory
robot to know where its arms are, since exact
positioning of components is a big part of its job.

We can tell where *our* limbs are because there's a
constant stream of messages from nerve fibres all
over our bodies telling us what's going on. Robots
have much simpler systems:

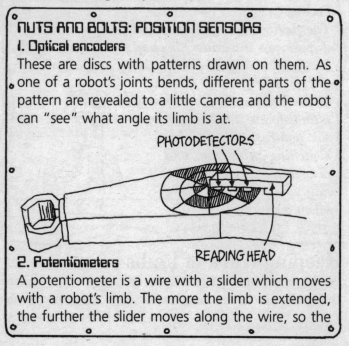

NUTS AND BOLTS: POSITION SENSORS

1. Optical encoders

These are discs with patterns drawn on them. As
one of a robot's joints bends, different parts of the
pattern are revealed to a little camera and the robot
can "see" what angle its limb is at.

PHOTODETECTORS

READING HEAD

2. Potentiometers

A potentiometer is a wire with a slider which moves
with a robot's limb. The more the limb is extended,
the further the slider moves along the wire, so the

more wire the electricity has to go through to complete its circuit. As the distance the electricity travels grows, the strength of the electricity falls, so the robot's computers can work out how stretched the limb is.

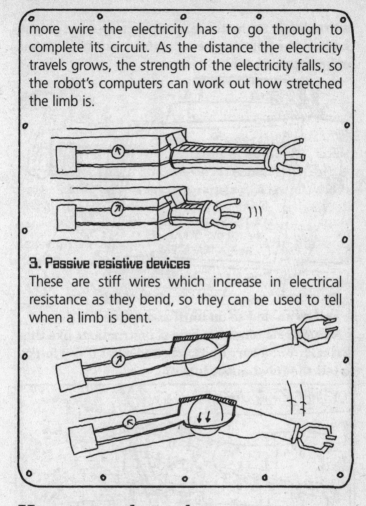

3. Passive resistive devices

These are stiff wires which increase in electrical resistance as they bend, so they can be used to tell when a limb is bent.

How to teach a robot

Factory robots need to do quite complicated things. There are two main ways to teach them – the hard way and the easy way!

The hard way is just to tell the robot what it's supposed to do by programming it with a list of instructions, for instance, a car-factory robot might be given the following set of instructions (translated into computer code):

... and so on and so on until about line 3,251.

But making immense lists of instructions like this is clearly not a very quick job, and what if you forgot to tell the robot about line 4?

So roboticists invented a really clever solution called direct teaching or lead-through programming, which means that people can now *show* a robot how to do a job like spray-painting a car. A switch is provided so that the human can switch the paint-jet on and off, and they simply spray a car themselves, using the spray-gun while it's still attached to the robot's arm. The arm's position sensors tell its computer exactly where the robot's arm is at each moment. Then the computer takes control, guiding the arm through the same positions again and switching the paint spray on and off just as the human did. So long as there's another car just where the last one was, the robot will spray it perfectly (or as perfectly as the human did, anyway). And, from then on, it can happily spray one car after another without making a mistake or getting bored.

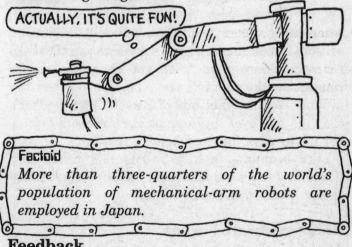

ACTUALLY, IT'S QUITE FUN!

Feedback

This is about the most fundamental robotic idea around (apart from "Why don't I get something else to do this boring job for me?"). Unlike most of the other bits of robotics, it's an idea that's been around for centuries. It's essential for modern factory robots, and it really just means passing information about how a task is going back to the thing that's doing the task, like someone telling a reversing motorist how they're doing by feeding back information about the car's position.

OK, STOP THERE!

You're packed with feedback systems yourself: when you put your foot down, lots of little internal sensors inside your leg send signals to your brain to tell you where your foot's got to, and pressure sensors on the sole tell you when it's reached the ground. We use other bits of ourselves for feedback too, like our eyes and our balance sensors (which are in our ears, for some bizarre reason).

Like humans, factory robots use touch and position sensors for feedback, but they don't make so much use of vision as we do.

Robot-restricted areas

A major advantage for a factory robot is that factories are nice and tidy, and robots HATE clutter. If something's not where it should be, or is where it shouldn't be, robots get into a bit of a tizzy (except the dumber ones, which just go on stacking non-

existent plates or
tightening not-there
screws). Clutter is
complicated, and
robots and their
programmers don't
want to spend time
and memory coping
with extra complication. That's why, in many ways,
humans and factory robots don't mix. Not only do
people clutter the place up with tea cups and shoes,
they are a bit vulnerable to being smacked on the
head by robot arms they weren't expecting.

At the moment, most factories that contain robots
contain people too. To cope, robots either need to:
a) have complex feedback systems built into them,
like advanced visual sensors which can spot people,
and enough intelligence to know how to avoid
hurting them
or
b) work in a cage.

In practice, it's often cheaper to...

But one way to make robots a bit safer is to install
a sense of touch – so they know to stop if they bang
into something or someone. So...

55

How do robots feel?

ALL COLD AND SMOOTH?

A BIT SICK AND DIZZY?

Actually, that's not *quite* what I meant...

For most robots, especially factory ones, touch is the most important sense, and even quite early models had a basic version.

NUTS AND BOLTS: TACTILE [TOUCH] SENSORS

1. Bump sensors

The good thing about touch sensors is that they can be very simple, like a bump switch. This is a little button or a feeler on a robot which tells it when it's driven into a wall. The switch sends an electrical signal to the robot's computer, which is programmed to recognize the signal as meaning an obstacle has been encountered. This is especially useful for mobile factory robots.

2. Electrostatic pressure sensors

To measure the pressure of its grip, a robot can have electric sandwiches fitted to its pincers or clamps or whatever else it uses for fingers. These are pairs of metal plates with special rubbery material called an elastomer in between. The more the robot crushes the material, the better the sandwich conducts electricity between the plates, so it's easy to work out how hard the robot is pressing from the strength of the current.

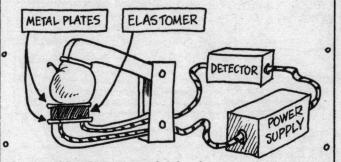

Sensors like this are useful for factory robots which have to move delicate items around.

3. Piezoelectrics

A piezoelectric material is one which generates electricity when it is squeezed, thumped, wobbled or heated, to give robots basic versions of a lot of the sensations we get from our skin. Many factory robots have several small chunks of piezoelectric material on their end effectors.

4. Robotic skin

It's possible to use lots and lots of tiny piezoelectric fragments to cover whole sections of robots to make artificial skin. Another type of artificial skin is a sheet of flexible rubbery plastic containing many tiny strands of wire. The strands change in electrical resistance when the skin is pressed by an object.

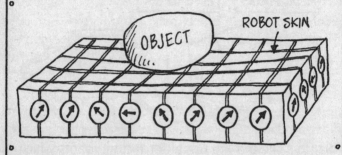

In practice, the complexity of these systems and the huge amount of computer power required for the robot to work out what's happening mean that robot skin isn't often used.

5. Thermal sensors

A very simple touch sensation for robots is temperature measurement – they're much better at this than people. All they need is an electronic thermometer. For factory robots which work in environments like welding shops, kilns or furnaces, temperature sensors can be used to warn them if they're getting too hot.

Robots on wheels

WEEEEEEEEE!

Mobile robots are much more complicated than ones that stay in one place – they need better senses, more complex computers, and on-board power systems as well as wheels, tracks or legs. So, until recently, people were still essential in factories to move things around. But robot technology is now advanced enough to allow full robotic mobility, which means that factories can be completely robotized.

Mobile industrial robots are called AGVs (Automatically Guided Vehicles), and are usually robotic trolleys or forklift trucks. They are particularly useful in frozen-food warehouses which are a bit parky for people, and in car factories where heavy parts need to be moved around.

Robomates

One of the bonuses about using groups of robots in factories and warehouses is that they can communicate very rapidly and reliably with each other and with computers. In automatic warehouses, robots keep the central computer posted on how many items are left, so the computer knows when it's time to order more.

Car factories often have six robots working on a car at the same time, and they do it quite happily without getting in each other's way. The idea of robotic teamwork has been investigated in detail over the last few years. At Reading University, for instance, there are seven small robots which work as a little team – their inventor, Professor Kevin Warwick, was unable to resist calling them the Seven Dwarves. They can follow a leader robot, herd people up, flock together or avoid each other. They scan each other using ultrasound and communicate with infra-red signals (see page 67). And they can do jobs together that they couldn't do individually, like moving big objects around.

HI-HO – HI-HO...

One reason for the amazing success of factory robots is that factory environments can be designed to be ideal for them to work in. But it's much more tricky for them to work in unpredictable, complicated, cramped, fragile places. Like households...

HOMEBOTS

Tidying your bedroom is really annoying, and if you don't think so, that just shows you haven't done it properly. Here we are, the human species, having spent millions of years evolving from little lumps of slimy jelly, and what do we spend our time doing? Making beds and picking up socks, that's what. Sickening, isn't it?

Being bored with housework isn't new of course, and people have been trying to invent machines to do it for them since they stopped having slaves. For many decades, people have hoped to have a humanoid robot that they could just tell to go shopping, wash the dishes, mow the lawn, and make them a nice cuppa, but none turned up. So, while they were waiting, people started to invent things that were halfway to robots. One of the first of these inventions was the vacuum cleaner, which has been around for well over 100 years. The electric washing machine turned up in 1908 and the pop-up toaster in 1919. None of these were much good to begin with – the vacuum cleaner needed constant pumping by a servant, the washing machine tended to electrocute people and the toaster shot burning bread round the kitchen.

So why don't we all have something more sophisticated by now?

Well, for one thing, though a fairly useful household robot could be built, it would just not be worth the money at the moment – it's all very well spending a few millions developing a robot to explore the universe, save lives or manufacture cheaper cars, but who's going to shell out that much for a machine to do the ironing and let the cat out? Why not just pay a human or two instead?

Of course, that hasn't stopped engineers from trying to build homebots: one of the first partially successful household robots was Tinker, which was built in 1966 and could do things like wash the car and vacuum the carpet. Ten years later there was Arok, which could vacuum, walk the dog, serve drinks and terrify people with the scary face its inventor gave it.

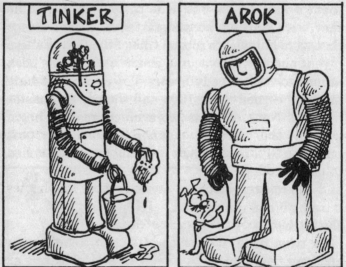

But, apart from the price (Arok cost about £30,000, more money than most of the houses it was

designed to clean), they took AGES to instruct: it
took four hours to program Tinker to wash each car.

One thing in particular that makes household
robots expensive and complicated is mobility. You
may think it's easy enough to run down stairs and
open the door, but that's because your house has
been designed for humans. It hasn't been designed
for robots to roll about in, unlike today's factories. A
lot of factory robots stand still and are fed their
work (cars to paint for instance) by a conveyor belt,
but a housebot would need to actually go and find
the bed it was supposed to make (and each time it
did, the bed would be in a different sort of mess). So
it's actually much easier for a robot to make a car
than a bed.

So, how can robots get around places like homes?

Robotic propulsion systems
If a robot has a nice smooth floor to travel around
on, and never needs to cope with stairs, wheels are
fine – they're speedy and easy to control. Most
mobile robots have either three, four or six wheels –

the more rugged the surface, the more they need. But more than 70% of the Earth's land surface is out of bounds to wheels – including a lot of your house (a mobile factory robot wouldn't even make it over the doorstep, never mind upstairs). Caterpillar tracks can cope with more rugged terrain, but they need a lot of space to turn in, so they're no good indoors (they can really ruin the carpet too). Spherical rolling robots are easy to build, but have no limbs to do anything with.

For extra-rugged landscapes – and stairs – there's really nothing like a nice set of legs. The exact number depends on what you want to do:

1. Monopods

One-legged research robots have been built and hop about quite rapidly, even over rough terrain. A monopod called Ricochet, built at the Leg Lab at the Massachusetts Institute of Technology, could move at 2.2 m per second. But there are a lot of jobs a one-legged robot can't do: painting, serving drinks, eye operations...

2. Bipeds

Some robots which have been built to imitate humans have two legs. But, like people, most aren't very stable – they need to balance themselves constantly, and if their power or brain is switched off in mid-step, they fall over. If you want to make a two-legged robot that won't fall over, it has to have very big feet and take very small steps, like Tinker.

3. Tripods and quadrupeds

Three or four legs are much more stable when the robot is standing still, but when it walks and one of its limbs is in the air, it tends to overbalance, like a stool or a table if you remove one of its legs. One of the first experimental quadruped puppet robots was a walking truck built for the US Army in the 1960s: any fewer than four legs would have been too unstable, any more than four, too complicated to control.

4. Hexapods

The best number of legs for a robot is six: three can be lifted together, leaving three on the ground to give a stable platform.

DADDY?

5. Multipods

Some robots have been built with even more legs – as many as 16. But the more legs a robot has, the more of its computer brain needs to be used to control them, the more power it needs, and the more moving parts there are to go wrong. And they don't help much anyway. An eight-legged robot that tried to walk like a six-legged one – by lifting four legs and leaving the other four in place – would be much more wobbly, just like a chair on a rough surface is wobbly but a three-legged stool isn't.

Factoid
Once a robot with legs has fallen over, it's very difficult for it to get up again. So if one attacks you, push it over and run. But don't try that with Genghis – it's a six-legged robot that is designed to chase any moving object, including you, and it's very hard to push over.

Outside research laboratories, there are very few robots with legs except for robotic pets like Aibos. Robotic brains aren't yet advanced enough to direct robots over the sort of complicated rugged terrain where legs come in really handy. And a walking robot consumes more than 20 times as much power as a wheeled one, because of the need to keep lifting its feet up.

A big challenge for a housebot is that its environment is full of all sorts of gubbins, from cups to kids to cats, and none of them likes being stepped on. So it needs to be able to detect them before it touches them, and the best way of doing that is by using:

NUTS AND BOLTS: PROXIMITY SENSORS

1. Some robots have little air jets built into them. When they approach an object, the air bounces back and sensors detect the increase in pressure.

2. Other robots generate electromagnetic fields, which they use like electric eels do. The fields are disturbed by nearby objects and generate electrical currents inside the robot – the problem is that the field is affected much more by a piece of metal than by a piece of wood, and a little magnet can seem as big as an iceberg.

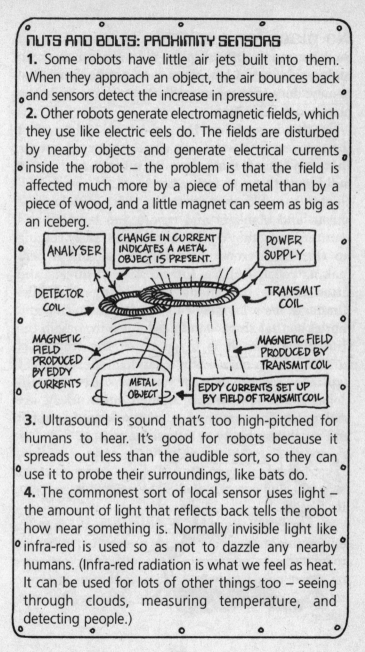

ANALYSER

CHANGE IN CURRENT INDICATES A METAL OBJECT IS PRESENT.

POWER SUPPLY

DETECTOR COIL

TRANSMIT COIL

MAGNETIC FIELD PRODUCED BY EDDY CURRENTS

MAGNETIC FIELD PRODUCED BY TRANSMIT COIL

METAL OBJECT

EDDY CURRENTS SET UP BY FIELD OF TRANSMIT COIL

3. Ultrasound is sound that's too high-pitched for humans to hear. It's good for robots because it spreads out less than the audible sort, so they can use it to probe their surroundings, like bats do.

4. The commonest sort of local sensor uses light – the amount of light that reflects back tells the robot how near something is. Normally invisible light like infra-red is used so as not to dazzle any nearby humans. (Infra-red radiation is what we feel as heat. It can be used for lots of other things too – seeing through clouds, measuring temperature, and detecting people.)

No place for a robot?

So, a house is a difficult place for a robot to work in, and sophisticated homebots may not be worth the money: does that mean we'll always have to do the housework ourselves?

No, thank goodness. But robots are only part of the answer: for a start, it's easier to invent houses that don't need much looking after than it is to build something to look after them. If people still slept in beds like they did in the 1950s with loads of sheets and blankets and covers and bolsters and counterpanes, they'd probably be constantly ringing up their local robot inventor to demand a bed-making robot. But the introduction of duvets and fitted sheets has made bed-making a doddle. Similarly, it's a lot easier to develop chemicals and fabrics so that shirts don't need much ironing in the first place than it is to go to all the trouble of building an enormously complicated and very expensive robot to do it for you. There are even self-cleaning windows which, though quite pricey, are still much cheaper than a window-cleaning robot and much less likely to fall on the cat.

Meanwhile, there are some household robots which cost less than a house and do a good job, but they're not the general-purpose humanoid servants we were all waiting for: they're 21st-century versions of 20th-century gadgets that vacuum, clear the table, mow the lawn in summer and blow the snow off it in winter, but they're all separate machines, each able to do only one job.

Factoid
By the end of 1999, about 3,000 household robots had been sold. The United Nations has predicted that by the end of 2003 there will be 290,000.

Butler-bots

Two new household robots appeared on the market in 2001: iRobot and R100. iRobot can climb the stairs, R100 can recognize your face and both can connect to the Internet (they use radio signals to do this, so they don't need to plug themselves in to phone sockets). They can also switch household appliances on and off with infra-red remote controls when you tell them to, or even when you email them from somewhere else (though if you don't treat R100 right, it's liable to say things like "What a Bother!").

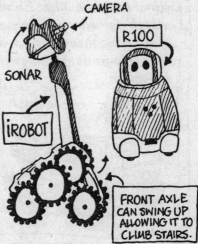

CAMERA

R100

SONAR

iROBOT

FRONT AXLE CAN SWING UP ALLOWING IT TO CLIMB STAIRS.

In future, as more and more household appliances get clever enough to operate remotely, it may be that household robots like more advanced versions of R100 and iRobot become common – but they will be much more like rather snooty butlers than household servants. Although you'll be able to email your robot to switch on the dishwasher, it will only be any good if you remembered to put the dishes in before you went out.

Factoid

A meat-eating robot was invented in Bristol in 1998, but it's fussy about its food and won't touch chicken. All it really likes is decomposing slug-flesh. SlugBot is designed to stop slugs eating garden plants and flowers by eating them instead. It's a 45-cm-square aluminium box, with wheels underneath and a 1.8-m arm on top. The arm has a three-fingered hand (equipped with a slime-scraper), and SlugBot has a camera to search for slugs. It recognizes their shapes by comparing them with copies in its memory bank, and if it finds one, it grabs it and puts it in its lunch box.

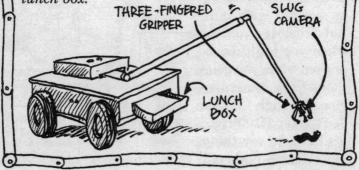

THREE-FINGERED GRIPPER

SLUG CAMERA

LUNCH BOX

> *It can catch a slug every six seconds, and when it's full up (or needs more power) it finds its way home using a combination of a global positioning system (see page 121) and an infrared camera. Back home it transfers the slugs to a chamber where they die and rot to produce some really smelly gas that is then burnt to provide SlugBot with electrical power.*

Smart homes

In the 1980s, Tokyo University started to develop an "Intelligent Home" called Tron, filled with thousands of computers, sensors and controls. If you lived in a Tron House, it would look after you by:

- delivering books or CDs to you from its underground library by means of small lifts
- using a video system in the kitchen to help you cook
- opening the windows when it's nice outside
- closing them when you turn the stereo on
- turning the stereo down when the phone rings
- giving you a health-check each time you go to the toilet.

But smart homes aren't perfect. When a visitor to the Tron House flicked what they thought was a light switch, the fire alarms went off and Tron

71

summoned the fire brigade. And sadly the designers hadn't included a "cancel" button...

Tron was an experimental smart home, but in Sweden some are now on the market, with the key to the system not being a massive computer or humanoid robot, but the fridge. The fridge has a touch-sensitive screen, so it's called a Screenfridge, and it:

- takes video messages for other people in the house
- warns you if you leave the cooker on or the freezer door open
- memorizes shopping lists
- suggests recipes based on what it's got on its shelves
- has a built-in phone, Internet connection, television and radio

oh, and...

- keeps food cool.

So, when you get round to buying your first household robot, maybe you'll be living in it...

MACHINES THAT THINK

There are well over a million robots in existence, so why don't we see more of them? Why don't we have lots of robotic rubbish collectors, street-sweepers or gardeners? People are great at inventing complicated machines and could easily build one that could make the movements needed to do all these things, so that's not the reason. In fact, robots already have bodies which are a lot better than ours in many ways – stronger, tougher, faster, tireless, and capable of more precise movements.

The problem is that robots are just not clever enough for those sort of jobs. The most advanced one couldn't out-think an earwig.

This sounds a bit strange – surely robots' computer brains are much more advanced than ours? Well, they are in some ways – they have better memories and can calculate much more rapidly than we can, but they're not intelligent. They're not imaginative or creative and they can't think up new ways of doing things or cope with unexpected situations.

That's why robots are mostly still confined to factories where they just follow instructions, and why they need to be remotely controlled when they do a human-like job such as bomb-disposal. And it's why the development of artificial intelligence (AI) is the biggest area of robotic research today: within a few years, robots may really start to think. And then there'll be no stopping them...

Can a machine think?
There are lots of arguments about what artificial intelligence really means and whether it's the same as human intelligence, but a simple definition is:

Artificial intelligence
A machine is artificially intelligent if it can do things that would require intelligence if done by a person.

things like...

Alan Turing, a scientist who worked in the 1940s and 1950s, came up with a test that would enable a person to tell if a machine is intelligent: if it can carry on a conversation (by email, say) with a person, so that the person thinks they're talking to another person, then this means the machine is intelligent.

So far, nobot has passed the Turing test, but they're getting closer.

Robots are sometimes classified by their intelligence levels, which are called generations:

1. First-generation robots literally just go through the motions, moving their limbs and grippers exactly as they're instructed to. Automata, simple robot toys, and Unimate are all first-generation robots. Some factory robots are first-generation too, but these days they're being replaced by...

2. Second-generation robots have sensors and the brain-power to react to what they detect. A second-generation egg-packer robot would be able to use visual sensors or touch sensors to detect that it had run out of eggs – or boxes – and would be clever enough to stop and ask for more. Second-generation robots still follow their programs though, and could never work out a new way of doing something.

3. Third-generation robots not only have sensors, they have some sort of intelligence too – not at a human level yet, but enough to allow them to learn things. A third-generation egg-packer might try out different ways of packing eggs to find out which way was quickest or used least cardboard. To do so, it would probably use trial and error – maybe quite a lot of error.

Third-generation robots have been under development since the 1960s. One of the first was Shakey, which used its two computer brains to help it explore a room containing simple objects and learn how to move them around: for instance, when it was asked to push a box off a platform it found a wedge-shaped block, pushed it against the platform and used the wedge as a ramp so that it could drive up on to the platform to get to the block.

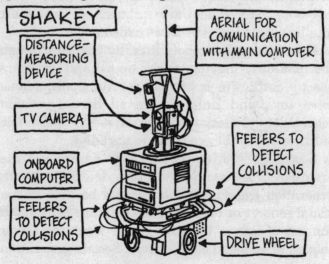

SHAKEY

DISTANCE-MEASURING DEVICE

AERIAL FOR COMMUNICATION WITH MAIN COMPUTER

TV CAMERA

FEELERS TO DETECT COLLISIONS

ONBOARD COMPUTER

FEELERS TO DETECT COLLISIONS

DRIVE WHEEL

How to make robots think

There are three main ways to make machines intelligent:

Knowledge-based robots

If a robot only has to understand one sort of thing – like how to play chess – then all it needs is the rules of the game and a powerful enough computer to work out all the possible outcomes of applying those rules. Then it can decide what to do to win the game. This is a knowledge-based system, and it can allow a machine to out-"think" a person – but only in its own special subject. When humans play against advanced chess-playing machines, they often feel as if they are competing against a living opponent.

Behaviour-based robots

The trouble is, there aren't many things in life that are controlled by sets of clear rules, so robots are often sent out into the cruel cold world to learn for themselves, equipped only with some rules of thumb

BUT I HAVEN'T GOT ANY THUMBS!

and the ability to modify those rules in the light of their experience – that is, they can learn from their mistakes (so long as they're not too fatal).

These are sometimes called "behaviour-based robots".

The first ancestors of these robots were built in 1948: Elmer and Elsie were two robot tortoises which could track down a light source, not bang into each other and go home when they got hungry (for electricity). They had rotating eyes, touch-sensitive feelers, two brain cells each, and surprised their inventor by dancing with each other*. Today's behaviour-based robots are capable of learning about their environment and adapting their behaviour to it.

Recently, a third type of intelligent robot has been developed, relying both on learned behaviour and programmed-in knowledge. One of these "hybrid" robots, called LUDWIG, has been built in Imperial College, London by Dr Murray Shanahan.

Factoid
Roboticists have used two approaches to making robots intelligent. The "top-down" approach tries to teach a robot how to use language or what the world is like. Shakey was taught like this. The

*Their inventor, William Grey Walter, called machines like this that behave like animals "Machina Speculatrix". Now they're called AL, for Artificial Life.

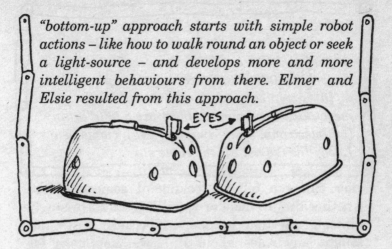

"bottom-up" approach starts with simple robot actions – like how to walk round an object or seek a light-source – and develops more and more intelligent behaviours from there. Elmer and Elsie resulted from this approach.

EYES

How to build a brain

Once a scientist has decided whether to use the top-down approach or the bottom-up one, they still need to choose the best way to "implement" it: that is, what sort of hardware they will use to actually build their artificial brain. Scientists who build knowledge-based systems normally choose ordinary (though very fast) computers, but many who prefer the bottom-up approach use machines with structures that are more like the human brain, called neural nets. As long ago as 1943, a bio-electric brain was constructed from jars of chemicals connected with metal plates. (Its designers couldn't use a computer because they hadn't been invented yet.) The brain learned to recognize simple patterns, and was called a neural net (or neural network), because it was a network of artificial neurons (brain cells). These days, neural nets are usually built by making a normal computer operate as if it is made of a network of tiny computers all linked together.

How can you tell by looking at someone's face whether they're male or female? It's a surprisingly difficult question to answer, because we're not taught any rules about it – we just learn for ourselves. But if you wanted to program a knowledge-based system to decide, you'd have to work out a set of rules and feed them in. A much easier, and more successful, way of solving the problem is by using a neural network. In a simplified way, it works like this:

As different faces are viewed by the camera, different patterns of electricity are generated. To begin with, the neural net is told the gender of each face, so that it can learn what types of electrical pattern are produced by male faces and what types are produced by female ones. Eventually, the net learns to judge the gender of the face for itself. Neural nets are about as good as we are at doing this, and they can learn to recognize individuals too. They are also used to forecast the weather, detect cancer cells, monitor electronic systems in aircraft and even predict oil prices.

Bladerunner is a 1982 film based on a book called *Do Androids Dream of Electric Sheep?* (Philip K Dick, 1968) which is about androids that can dream. This may really be possible: when neural nets are given a task to perform, you can tell they're working on it because of the flow of electricity around their circuits. In one of these systems, called MAGNUS, the electrical activity sometimes starts off by itself.

MAGNUS's designer, Professor Igor Aleksander, says that this is equivalent to dreaming. So maybe it's not impossible for a robot like Bender to dream about killing all humans...

Teambots

Another advantage that electronic brains have over meaty ones is that they have no feelings like boredom or jealousy. Combined with their excellent communication systems, this means that robots can work together very effectively to solve problems, and test out different solutions until they find the right one by trial and error. It might take a lot of goes though: in 1995, a group of robots finally learned to locate a white triangle from a set of clues, after trying 30 different methods they thought up, 29 of which were, not to put too fine a point on it, pants.

Robot relatives

There are lots of research projects going on at the moment to develop robots with human-like levels of intelligence. Rod Brooks, a scientist working at the Massachusetts Institute of Technology in the USA, has developed a humanoid robot called Cog. His approach is to allow Cog to develop its intelligence in the same way a human does: by interacting with people (it watches anyone who comes into the room) and "playing" with objects. He and his team have given it human-like hands and eyes so that it can do this. Cog is probably the most advanced AI robot in existence*.

Name: Cog
Function: AI research
Appearance: two-eyed, two-armed, no-legged humanoid
Date development started: 1993
Special abilities: learning like a human

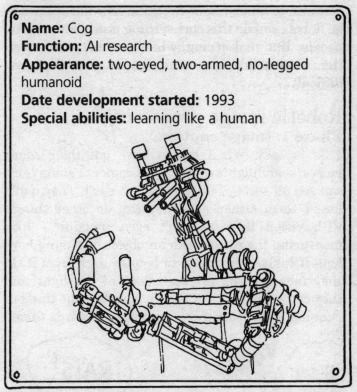

Watching, looking, seeing

Vision is very useful for robots for the same reasons it is for us: to find their way around, and to learn things (Cog learns largely through the use of vision). Sight is also a brilliant way of checking up on things without touching them – which is useful if the things to be checked are dangerous or fragile.

*Rod Brooks calls the type of AI Cog uses "subsumption architecture".

There is a very primitive sort of vision which is easy to install in a robot: using light to do something very specific, like measuring the distance to an object, or checking how flat a surface is. Robots can do this sort of thing much better than people. But real seeing, where a robot does more than simply taking a measurement, is much more difficult...

Robotic image processing
Phase 1: Image capture
This is easy. When robots have got their zoom lenses, searchlights or infra-red cameras going they can see all sorts of things that we can't. They don't forget them either, and they can do other things with vision that we can't even imagine – like measuring the distance to an object by timing how long it takes a light ray to bounce back from it. If they measure the precise colour of the light too, they can even work out exactly how fast the thing is running away from them or rushing towards them.

Also, their eyes are tough, they can have dozens of them if necessary, they can be connected to their hands or feet or anywhere else, and they can even be stuck on the wall and communicated with by radio. (DON'T TRY THIS WITH YOUR OWN EYE IF YOU'RE NOT A ROBOT.)

But, if you are a robot, switch off your smugness circuit, because phase 2, converting images into code, is very difficult. There's an enormous amount of information in a scene and a lot of it is constantly changing (especially if the viewer is moving).

Phase 2: Image analysis

The next thing robots do is to pick out distinctive features from the images – like edges or patches of equal brightness – and then group these features into sets of simple shapes.

That might sound easy, but actually it's still nearly impossible. So robots cheat. For instance, it's normally safe to say that a nice, clear shape which is all one colour and has a sharp edge all round it is an object. But unfortunately, that's what a lot of shadows look like, and they're not real objects at all. So robot users often do away with shadows by using diffuse lighting. They also sometimes use "structured light" – a pattern of lines of light (like those you get when the sun shines through a half-shut Venetian blind) that are projected over an object. The way the pattern is distorted lets robots work out the object's shape.

Some robots cheat even more by refusing to deal with anything that hasn't got a special computer-readable label on. This is very handy in factories, but of course it won't get them far in the real world.

Phase 3: Image understanding
Then there's the last stage of seeing: interpreting the code to work out what the object actually is. That's the real problem. Humans can recognize things because they're very clever and know all sorts of stuff. Look at this, for instance:

You can probably see this as a vase or as two faces. You can even *decide* which you want to see. You can do this because you know all sorts of things about vases and faces, and how they look from different angles. What a robot would make of it depends on how it's programmed: if it's designed to interact with people it would see faces, if it's an interior-design robot it would see a vase. If neither, it's likely to get confused.

To understand what images actually *are*, robots have to be artificially intelligent, which means they need:

a) huge libraries of different objects in their heads (or wherever they keep their brains)

plus

b) software that's clever enough to work out how all those objects look from different angles.

And then they have to compare very quickly what they see with that information.

And that's just the start. A rugby ball should be a very easy thing to identify – it has nice clear edges (unlike, say, a flame or a cloud), it's a simple shape that always looks either round or oval whatever angle it's viewed from, and there aren't all that many things around that can be confused with it. But it's not enough for a robot just to think, "Ah. Got it. A rugby ball." To do anything useful with that information, like play rugby, a robot would also need to know what a rugby ball does – which means not just the way rugby is played but also how objects move, spin and twist when they're kicked or rolled. Which means even bigger libraries and even faster software. Which is very tricky.

One of the most expensive and complex robots in the world looks even more human than Cog, and was designed to move around in a human-like way, climbing stairs, opening doors, and shaking hands. Yet it has no intelligence of its own at all. It seems almost human because it contains sophisticated balancing and feedback systems and can obey complicated sets of instructions. The Honda robot was developed secretly and stunned everyone when it was unveiled in 1996. It has gone through several versions, and the latest is called ASIMO.

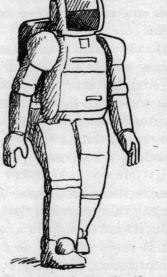

Name: Honda P1/P2/P3/ASIMO
Function: research robot
Appearance: humanoid
Date of first public appearance: 1996
Special abilities: climbs stairs, shakes hands, manipulates objects, sees in 3-D
Weaknesses: can only survive for 25 minutes without a recharge
Robot-spotters' notes: the most advanced self-contained (i.e. with on-board power supply and brain) robot around

BEAM robots

Most advanced research robots are highly complicated, and contain very fast computers, but there's a whole different approach to robot-building which doesn't use computers at all! Mark Tilden, a Canadian roboticist, has developed "nervous net" robots, which look like big insects. His robots, which have names like Unibug, VBUG and Spyder, use simple electronic circuits which control their insect-like legs. The circuits are designed to try out different solutions to a particular problem – like walking efficiently over rough terrain – and to select the most successful one. Mark Tilden's robots are very cheap to build compared to other robots, not only because they don't contain computers, but also because he often builds them out of scrap materials, like the motors from retired cassette recorders and bits of old camera. Robots like this are called BEAM robots (Biology, Electronics, Aesthetics and Mechanics*), and there are now annual Olympics in which BEAM robots climb

ropes, jump, swim and wrestle with each other. More recently, Dr Tilden has developed human-sized versions of his robots with saucer-shaped heads called Roswells.

Artificial intelligence allows a robot to do its job without needing to call on human beings for help. That's why it's most valuable in places where there are no human beings at all: like outer space.

*Sometimes other expansions of "BEAM" are used, like Biotechnology, Evolution, Analogue and Modularity.

SPACEBOTS

According to the telly, it won't be long before our descendants launch themselves into space, boldly going to distant star systems, often assisted by loyal robots like Data or not-so-loyal ones like Bender. They just click on *hyperdrive* and they're off. Well, maybe – in a few thousand years. For the foreseeable future though, interstellar journeys will take many human lifetimes, so a holiday on Altair IV isn't going to appear in the brochures for a while. And people need a great deal of looking after in space: they need heat, food, socks, drink, exercise, oxygen and light, and accelerations need to be kept low or they turn into mush.

Exactly. Robots don't get bored waiting a few dozen years for something to happen, they don't mind a bit of crushing acceleration, and they don't need water, oxygen or anything else except electricity. So they make far more suitable space-explorers than people. And they're a bargain too: it cost well over a billion pounds to get the first three people to the Moon in 1969, and that's as far as they went.

Robots, on the other hand, have explored all the planets in the solar system except Pluto, plus plenty of moons and the odd comet and asteroid, all for about fourpence (relatively speaking – the most advanced space robot mission, to Mars, cost about 265 million dollars, which is less than some Hollywood movies). So when it comes to space exploration, robots are a real bargain compared to you and me.

AND THAT'S IT, IS IT? NO OTHER REASON? NOT BECAUSE WE CAN BE LEFT IN SPACE?

Er ... well, yes. The other handy thing about space robots is that no one complains if you abandon them on Mars, not even the robot. In other words, they're expendable. Which saves all the money and effort of getting them back.

Since space exploration is such a suitable job for a robot, it's not surprising that NASA is one of the biggest investors in the development of sophisticated robots.

There are two categories of space robots: one type explores distant parts of space, from the Moon to the outer planets of the solar system, while the other works within a few thousand kilometres of the Earth (which is just round the corner, spacewise).

The Moon and beyond

There are three types of robot space-explorers – probes, landers and rovers...

Robot probes

These are sophisticated spacecraft, sent on missions to fly close to (or sometimes orbit) planets, moons and other bits of the solar system. Space probes are launched by rockets, and also use the gravity of planets to help them travel through space. What makes them robotic is that they're equipped with lots of special systems – like cameras, radar and radio receivers – to help them record data from the planets they go past, and they can adjust these systems without relying on the controllers on Earth. Robotically speaking though, they're quite primitive, without so much as a pneumatic hand or a cybernetic nose to pick with it. The difference between probes and more advanced space-explorer robots is that probes don't land anywhere.

Factoid
In 1962, Mariner 1, the first space probe, went off course and had to be destroyed – because a hyphen had been left out of its computer-coded instructions.

Four of the most impressive robotic probes were Pioneers 10 and 11 and Voyagers 1 and 2, which explored the outer planets of the solar system in the 1970s and 1980s. The Voyagers were the most advanced.

They had cameras which were sensitive to visual light, ultraviolet and infra-red, and they could also detect charged particles, magnetic fields, cosmic rays and weird space gas called plasma. They used radioactive material to provide them with power and also had 16 little gas jets each, which they squirted in different directions so they could move themselves around for a bit of sightseeing. Mostly what they were looking at were MASSIVE planets, and they sent some excellent electronic postcards of them back to Earth.

They're all still out there, beyond the furthest planet, occasionally sending signals back to us. And they're not alone. The Huygens probe is on its way to explore a weird moon of Saturn called Titan. Titan is always shrouded in clouds containing gases like those life on Earth developed from. Huygens will measure temperature, wind speed and gas types on its way down. It's a bit cold for life as we know it to exist there, but we don't really know what Huygens will have to cope with when it lands, in 2004.

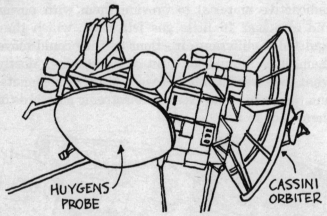

HUYGENS
PROBE

CASSINI
ORBITER

A probe called Stardust was launched in 1999, to visit a comet called Wild Two in 2004. It will fly through the comet's coma – the cloud of dust and gas that surrounds the comet's core – and collect samples. It should return the dust to Earth in January 2006. The probe Deep Impact may visit the core of a comet called Tempel 1 in 2005, drill a hole in it and return to Earth with whatever it finds.

Landers

Landers are more advanced than probes. They are equipped with all sorts of robotic sense-organs, from cameras and earthquake detectors to "noses" that can sniff out interesting chemicals, and some have arms to scoop up bits of whatever planet they've been sent to. They have explored Venus, the Moon and Mars, and the most advanced ones were the twin Vikings.

No – not them. The Viking Landers touched down on Mars in 1976. They didn't have any legs or wheels, so they had to stay where they landed, but each had a TV camera to send pictures back to Earth, and an extendible arm with a scoop and a magnet on the end (plus a little brush to clean the magnet with).

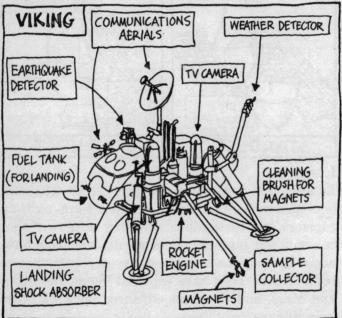

VIKING

COMMUNICATIONS AERIALS

WEATHER DETECTOR

EARTHQUAKE DETECTOR

TV CAMERA

FUEL TANK (FOR LANDING)

CLEANING BRUSH FOR MAGNETS

TV CAMERA

ROCKET ENGINE

SAMPLE COLLECTOR

LANDING SHOCK ABSORBER

MAGNETS

The Vikings used their arms to scoop up Martian soil, before eating and digesting it by dissolving it in different liquids. Earth scientists hoped the results of the digestion would reveal evidence of life on Mars – but they didn't. Well, probably not: there was a lot of weird hissing and sizzling, but most scientists now think it was the result of strange soil chemicals rather than Martian bugs.

Crunchbots

There are also robots that are half-lander and half-probe. They don't land on planets, but they don't fly past them either. Instead, they ...

... sadly. They often get brilliant close-up photos on the way down though.

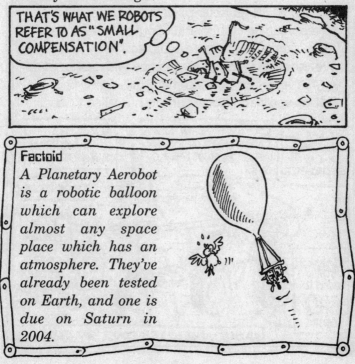

Factoid

A Planetary Aerobot is a robotic balloon which can explore almost any space place which has an atmosphere. They've already been tested on Earth, and one is due on Saturn in 2004.

Robot rovers

Rovers are landers equipped with wheels or caterpillar tracks to help them get around and explore. So far, there have been three of these, two on the Moon and one on Mars. Sojourner, the rover which landed on Mars in 1997 after a seven month, 192,000,000-km voyage, was a real robotic hero, even though it did look like a skateboard.

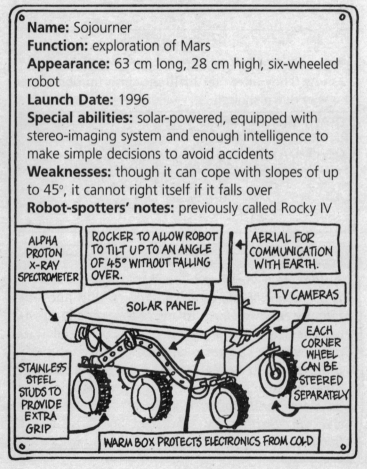

Name: Sojourner
Function: exploration of Mars
Appearance: 63 cm long, 28 cm high, six-wheeled robot
Launch Date: 1996
Special abilities: solar-powered, equipped with stereo-imaging system and enough intelligence to make simple decisions to avoid accidents
Weaknesses: though it can cope with slopes of up to 45°, it cannot right itself if it falls over
Robot-spotters' notes: previously called Rocky IV

ALPHA PROTON X-RAY SPECTROMETER

ROCKER TO ALLOW ROBOT TO TILT UP TO AN ANGLE OF 45° WITHOUT FALLING OVER.

AERIAL FOR COMMUNICATION WITH EARTH.

SOLAR PANEL

TV CAMERAS

STAINLESS STEEL STUDS TO PROVIDE EXTRA GRIP

EACH CORNER WHEEL CAN BE STEERED SEPARATELY

WARM BOX PROTECTS ELECTRONICS FROM COLD

Sojourner's first challenge was to survive the landing – its spacecraft was travelling at 7.6 km per second when it hit the atmosphere of Mars, and it had to lose speed so rapidly that Sojourner became 40 times heavier than on Earth for a while – something no human astronaut could survive. Once it was safely on the surface of Mars, Sojourner drove around on six wheels, making simple decisions like which way to go round obstacles. It sent 3-D images back to Earth, and analysed Martian rocks with its excitingly named Alpha Proton X-ray Spectrometer, which worked out what they were made of by blasting them with X-rays and making exact measurements of the radiation they gave off in response.

Other robot rovers are currently being built by NASA, like Nomad, which is 1.8 m long and has been developed for future unmanned space missions. It's been tested in Antarctica, and it is even clever enough to do nothing – just what needs doing when you've been given a dodgy instruction. It has an arm, a camera and a device that can determine the chemicals in rock samples – very handy if you're looking for meteorites, which is what Nomad has been used for. It was trained by being shown samples of real meteorites and things which looked like meteorites but weren't ("meteowrongs", they're wittily called), and it managed to find bucketsful of the right sort.

So robots are ideal for exploring space. But that doesn't mean it's an easy job – there are plenty of problems that robotic space explorers have to face:

Problem 1: Time delay

Normally, when things get tricky for a robot it can just shrug its titanium-reinforced shoulders and ask its human controller for help. But a space robot can't do this – it has to make urgent decisions itself. That's because of two things: space and light.

The problem with space is that there's such a lot of it about. It's a very long way from London to New York, but it's half a million times further to Neptune, the most distant planet investigated by a space probe. This means that, although light is thousands of times faster than the fastest space ship, it still takes quite a while to cross the spaces between the planets: four and a half hours to get to Neptune for instance. Radio messages travel at the same speed as light does, and that causes a problem.

Imagine you're a T-bot called Bill.

101

④ One day you're trundling along in your robotic way straight towards a VOLCANO!

—TRUNDLE!

⑤ Images from your camera are being beamed back to Earth...

NEPTUNE

EARTH

⑥ ...where Mission Control scientists are happily watching out for Tritonian aliens.

BETS | 10% |
ODDS | 6/4 |
100-1 | 14/1 |

⑦ More than four hours after your camera picks up the scary volcano ahead, the signals reach Earth and—

STOP

⑧ The signal makes its way back to Triton, taking another four and a half hours to get there, by which time you're lying in little pieces all over the place, having been blasted out of existence by the volcano and nibbled by Tritonians.

Which is all very irritating.

Whatever the scientists do, they can't get those signals to Bill any quicker: you just can't beat the speed of light. So the only answer is to get Bill to make the decision, rather than Mission Control on Earth. So Bill needs to be artificially intelligent, like Sojourner was.

Even when there aren't any disasters looming, puppet robots aren't much good in space: normally, when messages take a long time to get through to remote-control robots, the robots are programmed to "report and wait" until the messages they send have had time to go back to control and the control signal to come back to the robot. For a robot on Mars this would mean it spent up to 40 minutes waiting for each response! It's not much fun for the operator either – humans find it difficult to operate things like robot hands by remote control if there is a delay of more than about a tenth of a second between them instructing the hand to move and the hand moving. This means that a human would have difficulty controlling a T-bot even on the Moon.

Problem 2: Power

Ask most robots what they do for power and they'll say: "_____". But that's only because they're no good at speech recognition yet. What they all like is electricity, but where they get it from and what they do with it are slightly trickier questions. Most of them get their power from the mains, either directly or via rechargeable batteries (so if you're a robot and you ever fancy dominating the earth and wiping out humanity, make sure they've left the power on first).

WE'LL NEVER CONQUER THIS STUPID PLACE NOW!

I'M FEELING PECKISH!

Mains power is fine unless robots have to work a long way from a mains socket – like out in space, say. In that case, a little atomic power cell, which generates electricity from the energy produced by decaying radioactive* materials, is very handy. They've often got solar panels as well. Scientists are developing new fuel cells too, which produce electricity from chemical reactions.

Once a robot has its electricity supply, there are three ways it can use it: to power electric motors, or to pump either compressed air or oil to the joints they want to move†. Which way is best depends on the robot's job: hydraulic (oil-filled) joints are

*Radioactivity is either a type of intense radiation, a stream of high-speed particles or a mixture of both that is released naturally by some materials and can also be made artificially.
†The bits that make a robot move are called its actuators.

powerful (but noisy), pneumatic (air-filled) ones are
fast and light and electric ones are accurate.

Most robots cope with the power-source problem
by carrying electric batteries with them, recharged
by solar panels. One of the first rovers, Lunokhod 2,
had these.

TV CAMERA

SOLAR PANELS

MAGNETIC-FIELD DETECTOR

3D TV CAMERA

But solar panels are fragile, unwieldy, don't work
well far out in space or at night, don't supply a lot
of power, and get dusty. A solar-powered robot with
dusty panels is stuck until humans – or robots –
arrive with a duster or a charger.

And solar-powered robots need to spend a *lot* of
time sunbathing.

ANOTHER CHILLED OIL, PLEASE.

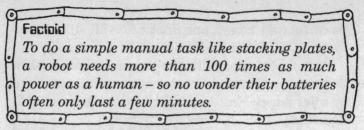

Problem 3: Self-repair

This has been the biggest problem with space robots. Lots of them – including Sojourner – have just stopped working because some crucial bit of them went wrong, and even the most advanced can do very little to repair themselves. But then people aren't too great at that either.

OH, NO, NOT THE DRILL!

WIZZZ zzzz...!

About all that can be done is to provide the robot with backup systems that it can switch to if the main ones stop working.

Problem 4: The unexpected

As well as the problems roboticists know about already – time delay, lack of power, lack of repair facilities – there are plenty they can't anticipate, unexplored planets being what they are.

For instance, when the Venera 14 lander arrived on the planet Venus in 1982, it was supposed to use its robotic arm to scoop up a sample of soil. But when the lander discarded its cover – which it was meant to do – sadly it landed in *exactly* the place where the soil sample was being taken, so the arm sampled the cover, instead of a nice lump of Venus.

One day people will probably get to Mars – although robots will be sent there first, to get things ready for them. But humans probably won't get any further out in space than that, at least for many decades – the cost of a human Mars mission will be enormous, and to get to the next really interesting place, the moons of Jupiter, would take far more time and money, since they're about ten times as far from Earth. So Mars may be the last planet humans set foot on. But, within a few years, advanced artificially intelligent robots will allow us to feel as if we're walking wherever a robot walks – we'll be able to link our senses with those of robot space explorers and feel and see and hear what distant planets are like. (This is called a virtual-reality system.)

Close to home

There are four types of space robots which are designed to work just beyond the Earth's atmosphere: manipulators, robonauts, space surveillance systems and robot shuttles.

The RMS

What has eight eyes, can move objects as big as small planes and is twice as long as a bus?

Correct. The RMS is a massive robot with an arm. In fact, it is an arm, the longest robotic arm in the world at 15 m, which folds out from a Space Shuttle.

It's used to grab satellites and other bits of space kit, and it's equipped with a computer that tells it the best way to get the job done, eight cameras, a shiny coat to keep it cool, a heating system to stop it getting cold, and it can be jettisoned into space if it goes wrong.

Robonauts

Under development by NASA, these are artificially intelligent humanoid robots which could be used in human environments in space, like inside space stations. These areas have been designed for the human body to access, so when there are no humans around and the stations need servicing, the best shape for a repair robot is humanoid.

Factoid

Robonauts can exist as happily in space as in space ships, so they can quickly be sent outside to deal with a problem: meanwhile, it takes a human being at least three hours to get into a spacesuit.

Space surveillance

Aercams (Autonomous Extravehicular activity Robotic CAMeras) are little self-powered spherical cameras equipped with nitrogen thrusters to jet them around in space. They're about 35 cm across and they're used to keep an eye on space-stations and shuttles.

NOBODY MESSES WITH MY SPACE STATION

Factoid

NASA estimates that by 2004, 50% of the activity originally carried out by astronauts outside their spacecraft will be done by robots instead.

Robot shuttle

The first robot ship was much bigger than an Aercam, and took off in 1978. It was called Progress 1, and its job was to behave as far as possible as if it had a crew on board.

SO IT MADE SILLY JOKES AND THREW UP A LOT?

Progress 1 was a Soviet ferry ship (or shuttle craft, as they call them on *Star Trek*), which could dock automatically with a Soviet space station, controlling its own course by manipulating its rockets and retro-rockets, and guiding itself by means of a radio-link with its target. It carried things like orange juice, a new TV and spare socks for the cosmonauts. Not only that, it also used its own power to nudge the space station into a higher orbit. So it was a highly successful space robot. As a reward it was ...

... filled with rubbish and allowed to burn up in the Earth's atmosphere. What was left fell into the Pacific Ocean.

If the wreckage of Progress is ever found, it will probably be by a robot from the next chapter...

SEABOTS

You might think the sea is quite fun, and all you have to worry about is jellyfish. But go further in, and it gets a bit dodgy – it's dark, cold, full of sudden currents and weird fish with glowing eyes and massive teeth. And of course there's not a lot to breathe down there and the pressure increases rapidly the deeper you go (10 m down it's double what it is on the surface, 20 m down it's three times higher). But there are jobs that need to be done down there – things like scraping barnacles off the undersides of ships, digging about in the sand to find cables that need repairing, collecting lumps of metal (which is the undersea equivalent of mining) and prospecting for oil and gas. Not much fun? Dangerous? Boring? This is a job for: an underwater robot.

There are thousands of underwater robots and they're used for all sorts of jobs. The simplest ones have no arms and are linked by cable to their controllers, so they can only be used to inspect things like fish, pipes and cables. More advanced versions have their own power sources and guidance systems and are used for mapping the sea floor, while some have grippers and can be used for tasks like cable-laying, exploration and welding.

Underwater robots are very popular with North Sea oil companies, the nuclear industry uses them to look at the bits of its reactors it keeps underwater, and NASA sends them out to retrieve the discarded rocket boosters of space shuttles.

Factoid

The biggest underwater robot, a Remote Maintenance Vehicle built by Shell, weighs 35 tonnes and is as big as a double-decker bus.

THIS ISN'T PECKHAM HIGH STREET!

Amazingly enough, the first underwater robot was built over 100 years ago. It was a radio-controlled submersible boat built by an electrical genius called Nikola Tesla and it was first demonstrated in the United States in 1898.

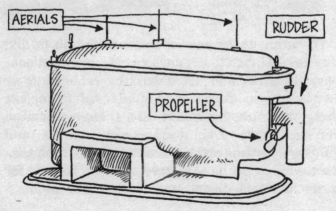

AERIALS

RUDDER

PROPELLER

However, it was many decades before underwater robots became advanced enough to do any useful work, because the underwater environment is such a tricky place to cope with (even for people). The first salvage (recovery) robots were used by the US navy in the early 1960s: in 1966 a heroic one called Cable-controlled Undersea Recovery Vehicle I (CURV I) managed to retrieve a lost hydrogen bomb from nearly a kilometre deep, so far down that human divers would have been crushed by the pressure.

Factoid

One thing that makes underwater life much more difficult for a human than a seabot is that a human has to spend many hours "decompressing" after a deep dive – if they return straight to the surface, gas bubbles form in their blood and they die horribly. Robots have no such problem.

By the 1970s underwater puppet robots were being used to weld oil pipes, and an advanced underwater robot called JTV-1 was built in the early 1980s. It was a Japanese remote-controlled machine which could move around and look at things with its TV cameras – things like shoals of fish and pipelines. Soon after, JTV-2 explored Antarctica in search of weird sea creatures and underwater cables. Underwater puppet robots like these are called ROVs – Remotely Operated Vehicles.

To cope with such a complicated environment, robots like JTV-1 have to have special features and be able to cope with extreme conditions:

ROBOT'S REALM

Rust is a fairly easy problem to solve, but there's a much bigger challenge that underwater robots face:

Talking through water

It's much harder to communicate in water than out of it. The trouble is, radio waves don't travel through water, so you have to use sound waves instead. But they're slow, have fairly short ranges, and can't carry much information: great for the simple things that whales need to chat about, but a bit limited for robots.

So underwater robots normally either have to surface so that they can communicate with their controllers by radio, or be connected by cables to computers and people. One robot that could be connected either to a ship or a submarine was Jason Junior, probably the most famous underwater robot of all.

Jason Junior explored the *Titanic* in 1986 after another ROV, Argo, had found the ship the previous year.

Name: Jason Junior
Function: underwater explorer
Appearance: boxy framework with LOADS of lights on front
Date: 1986
Special abilities: highly manoeuvrable. Can operate at depths of 61,000 m
Weaknesses: armless

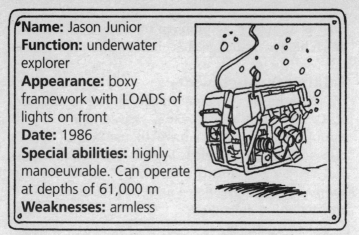

Jason was a T-bot, attached either to a boat or to a submarine called Alvin by an 80-m cable. Being armless meant it couldn't do much more than have a look at things, but when it did need to get to grips with objects, like old bits of *Titanic*, another underwater robot called Knuckles was attached to it. The robots were used together again in 1989 to bring up ancient pots from a sunken ancient Greek ship called *Isis*.

Name: Knuckles
Function: underwater robotic arm system
Appearance: system of rods with gripper
Date: 1986
Special abilities: works with Jason Junior
Weaknesses: can't be used independently

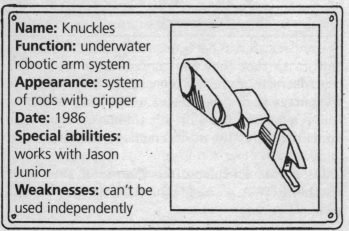

JASON AND KNUCKLES

CABLE

CAMERA WITH FLASH

SONAR

TV CAMERA

THRUSTER

KNUCKLES

GRIPPER

Seabots don't always get glamorous jobs like that though: they can also be used to scrape barnacles from ships' bottoms. If you've ever been near a ship's bottom when it's in need of a good scraping, you can imagine what an unpleasant job that is.

"GO TO SEA" THEY SAID, "IT'LL BE FUN" THEY SAID...

But Marine Robot RM3 does the job in no time. Well, actually in quite a lot of time: it only moves at 2.5 cm a minute. But who cares? It can be left to get on with it by itself while you do something more important like perfecting your tea-making skills.

Any robot that can move around needs to navigate, and for land robots there are several methods to choose from:

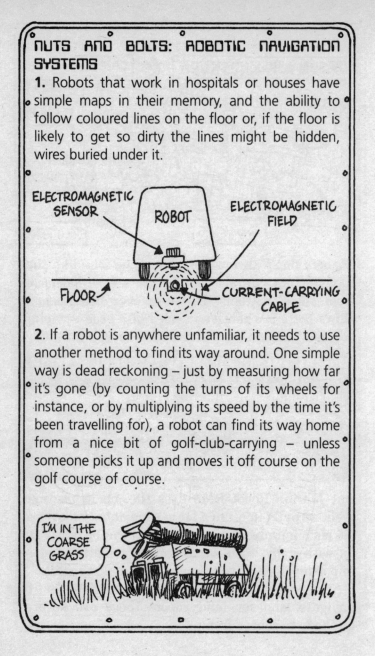

NUTS AND BOLTS: ROBOTIC NAVIGATION SYSTEMS

1. Robots that work in hospitals or houses have simple maps in their memory, and the ability to follow coloured lines on the floor or, if the floor is likely to get so dirty the lines might be hidden, wires buried under it.

ELECTROMAGNETIC SENSOR

ROBOT

ELECTROMAGNETIC FIELD

FLOOR

CURRENT-CARRYING CABLE

2. If a robot is anywhere unfamiliar, it needs to use another method to find its way around. One simple way is dead reckoning – just by measuring how far it's gone (by counting the turns of its wheels for instance, or by multiplying its speed by the time it's been travelling for), a robot can find its way home from a nice bit of golf-club-carrying – unless someone picks it up and moves it off course on the golf course of course.

I'M IN THE COARSE GRASS

Dead reckoning can be used for underwater robots, but only roughly because they're surrounded by moving water so they can't accurately measure their true speed.

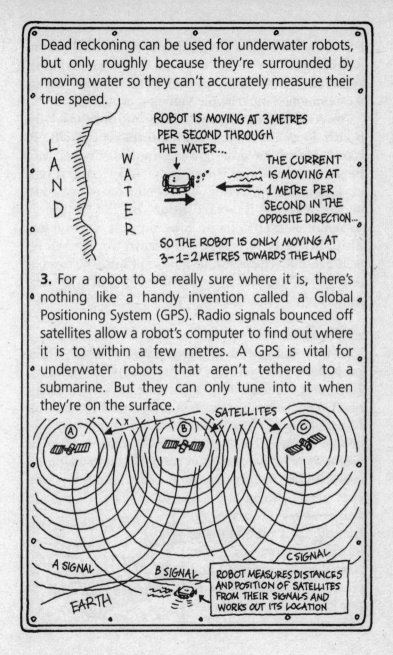

ROBOT IS MOVING AT 3 METRES PER SECOND THROUGH THE WATER...

THE CURRENT IS MOVING AT 1 METRE PER SECOND IN THE OPPOSITE DIRECTION...

L
A
N
D

W
A
T
E
R

SO THE ROBOT IS ONLY MOVING AT 3 − 1 = 2 METRES TOWARDS THE LAND

3. For a robot to be really sure where it is, there's nothing like a handy invention called a Global Positioning System (GPS). Radio signals bounced off satellites allow a robot's computer to find out where it is to within a few metres. A GPS is vital for underwater robots that aren't tethered to a submarine. But they can only tune into it when they're on the surface.

SATELLITES

Ⓐ Ⓑ Ⓒ

A SIGNAL   B SIGNAL   C SIGNAL

EARTH

ROBOT MEASURES DISTANCES AND POSITION OF SATELLITES FROM THEIR SIGNALS AND WORKS OUT ITS LOCATION

So, equipped with a navigation system and a power source, an underwater robot can cope without being tethered. These free-swimming robots are called Autonomous Underwater Vehicles, or AUVs.

An AUV called Autosub is being developed by Southampton Oceanography Centre in the UK. It has to carry its own power supplies – seven car batteries which give it a range of 70 km. And it has several sensors to tell it what's going on: an attitude sensor checks its orientation in the water, a pressure sensor tells it how deep it is, and an altitude sensor tells it how far down the sea bed is, so it can map the ocean floor. One of Autosub's tasks will be to monitor the effects of global warming underneath the polar ice-caps.

Autofish

The way fish swim is much more efficient than propellers, oars, paddles or anything else we know. How they manage it is a bit of a mystery – they don't seem to have enough muscle power to move as fast as they do (this is so odd that the mystery has got a name: Gray's Paradox – named after a zoologist who discovered in the 1930s that dolphins seemed to have only about one-seventh of the power they need to swim at the speeds they do). So robotic fish have been constructed to study this problem: one of the first was a robot tuna, built in 1994, and since then other types of fish, and a robotic lobster, have also been invented to

help us understand their living counterparts and to develop more energy-saving ways of moving through water (already robot fish use less than half the energy propellers do to reach the same speed).

There are plans to make robotic versions of extinct sea creatures too, which could then be put in zoos. And you can already buy an underwater robotic pet jellyfish called an Aquaroid, which is a lot easier to look after than a real one. Aquaroids glow, dance, react to each other and to human voices, and never ever try to sting you to death.

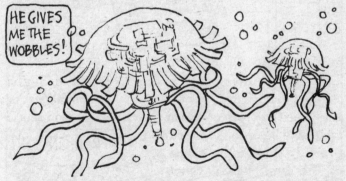

The underwater world is a difficult place for robots to work in, but it's positively comfy compared to some of the places robots have to put up with, as we'll see in the next chapter.

HAZBOTS

WARNING: DO NOT LET YOUR ROBOT READ THIS CHAPTER IF IT IS OF A NERVOUS DISPOSITION

Sometimes, jobs are given to robots not because they're strong or tough or waterproof, but because they're expendable: if it's a choice between a robot being blown to bits or a person, it will be the robot that ends up in a sad pile of cogs on the floor. There is no shortage of jobs like that for robots to do:

There are some hazards that are no problem for robots – like cold or airlessness. But often, what is bad for a person is bad for a robot too – like fire or explosions. What makes it even more difficult is that hazard robots (or hazbots, as they're sometimes called by sci-fi types) must be much more reliable than factory robots or household robots, because if they go wrong it's not easy to go and fix them. The robot's brain can be kept a long way from the robot itself, so at least it can be got at easily if it goes wrong (and if the worst happens and the robot gets...

it can be re-used).

Robots that go to dangerous places haven't been around very long, because the places where they have to go are exactly the sort they don't handle too well: they're unpredictable, complicated, and full of things to trip over. So robots had to wait until they were clever enough to make sense of a hazardous environment. But now the technology is advanced enough to cope.

Radioactive robots

Radioactive environments are the easiest for hazard robots to cope with – the radiation doesn't bother them a bit, in fact a lot of space robots eat it for breakfast (see page 104). People, on the other hand, die in a variety of horrible ways if they're exposed to too much radiation: from burns, radiation sickness or cancer. So it's not surprising that the earliest hazard robots were used in nuclear plants (see page 22). These days though, they're swimming around nuclear reactor cores, helping to make closed-down plants safe and patrolling dangerously radioactive areas. The UK's Atomic Energy Authority, for example, has got robots on caterpillars...

YEEE-HAH!

caterpillar *tracks* called Spider and Roman, and there's also a giant robotic tentacle called Links which can explore the insides of reactors.

LINKS

VIEWING WINDOW

CONCRETE SHIELD

END EFFECTOR

One of the most dangerously radioactive areas on earth is the remains of the Chernobyl nuclear plant in the Ukraine, where the worst ever nuclear accident took place in 1986. Any collapse of the ruins is likely to release even more deadly radioactive materials into the atmosphere, so since 1999 an advanced hazbot called Pioneer has been used to patrol the site, scanning for collapsing areas which it marks on 3-D computer maps. It also measures radiation and heat levels. Pioneer is equipped with a gripper and a plough attachment which allow it to clear rubble. Its design is based on the Sojourner Mars-exploring robot (see page 98).

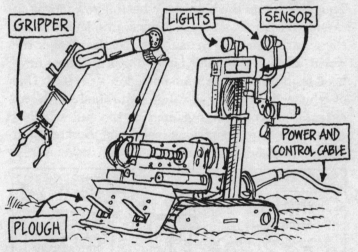

GRIPPER

LIGHTS

SENSOR

POWER AND CONTROL CABLE

PLOUGH

Bombots

Bomb disposal robots have been around since 1975, and started off in Northern Ireland. So far they're all puppet robots or T-bots, as some people feel it might be a bit unsafe to let a robot make up its own mind about how to cope with a bomb.

The first was Wheelbarrow, which disposed of bombs by shooting them with a shotgun. It was equipped with a TV camera that relayed pictures back to its human controllers.

Though a bit on the big side, Wheelbarrow moves on caterpillar tracks and can climb stairs. Hundreds of them have been sold to deal with bombs all over the world. Recently, smaller bomb-disposal robots have been built that can be transported in a car boot. One of these is Hobo, a robot equipped with an extendible arm with a gripper on the end, which it uses to pick up suspicious-looking objects and put them down somewhere safe.

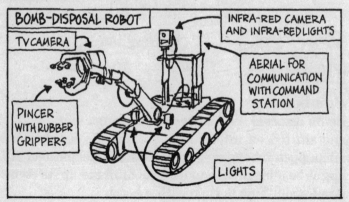

BOMB-DISPOSAL ROBOT

INFRA-RED CAMERA AND INFRA-RED LIGHTS

TV CAMERA

AERIAL FOR COMMUNICATION WITH COMMAND STATION

PINCER WITH RUBBER GRIPPERS

LIGHTS

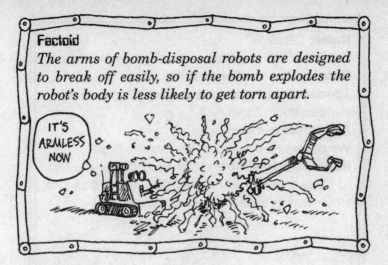

Hotbots

Robots have been designed to cope with natural hazards too, not just man-made ones. And nature doesn't get much scarier than...

These days it's possible to predict when volcanoes will do their stuff, but ideally that requires someone to wander about dangerously near the crater taking measurements. Someone or something...

...like Danté, an eight-legged T-bot, named after the author of a book about a volcanic hell under the Earth.

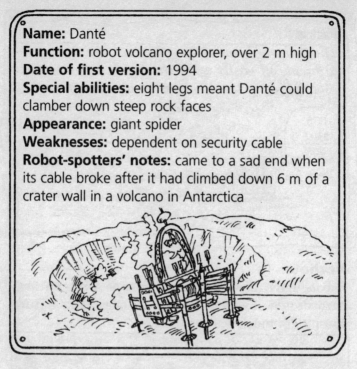

Name: Danté
Function: robot volcano explorer, over 2 m high
Date of first version: 1994
Special abilities: eight legs meant Danté could clamber down steep rock faces
Appearance: giant spider
Weaknesses: dependent on security cable
Robot-spotters' notes: came to a sad end when its cable broke after it had climbed down 6 m of a crater wall in a volcano in Antarctica

The next version, Danté II, scrambled all over an Alaskan volcano, and measured gas temperatures too.

Sadly:

Happily:

Unhappily:

Firedroids

Robot fire-fighters are becoming so popular, there's
now an annual fire-fighting competition for them in
which they have to respond to a fire alarm, move
through a mock-up of a house until they've found
the fire, and then put it out. Robots make good fire-
fighters in that they don't need to breathe and can
see through smoke using ultrasound. They can cope
with a certain amount of heat too, but they can't get
really hot or their circuitry will melt. So they keep
cool like we do: by sweating. Water is pumped over
their surfaces through a system of tubes, and as it
evaporates it carries away some of the heat with it.
Fire-fighting robots also have to cope with lots of
smoke and dust, which they manage by blowing air
out of every opening.

But there's a limit to what even the toughest robot
can cope with, so they have to use brain-power to
help them: intelligent fire-fighting robots can plot a

safe-ish route through a dangerous area by selecting the best compromise between the coolest path and the quickest one.

One recent hazard robot is Robug-3, an eight-legged, wall-climbing machine, which can find its way through smoke using ultrasound, and is equipped with an arm and a hose. It's already been used to help in real fires.

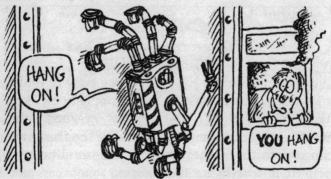

132

Nosebots

We drone on about the odour of freshly baked bread, the tang of rain, or the smell of that bottle of milk we left in the back of our desk drawer last year. But most robots don't need to smell anything to do their jobs so most of them don't have robo-noses. But it's a very useful skill for hazard robots that might want to detect smoke, explosives, radioactive gas or methane (which you may have sampled if you've ever lingered about behind a cow).

SNIFF! SNIFF!

Just like touch or sight, it's very easy to make a machine that can answer specific questions like "is that surface flat?", "have I just crashed into a wall?", or "is that smoke I can smell?" So that's what smell-detecting robots do – just answer simple is-it-or-isn't-it questions about smells.

133

NUTS AND BOLTS: AROMA ANALYSIS

1. Some things are very simple to sniff out:

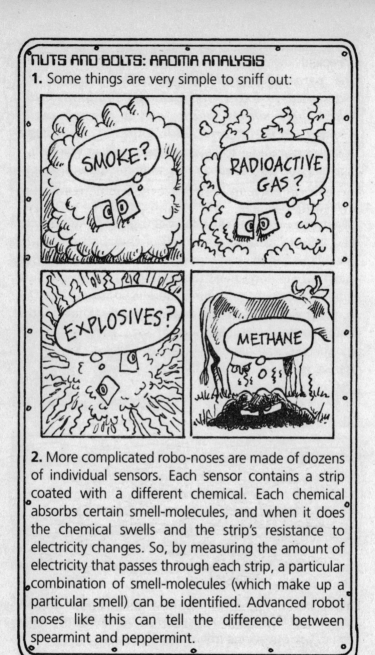

2. More complicated robo-noses are made of dozens of individual sensors. Each sensor contains a strip coated with a different chemical. Each chemical absorbs certain smell-molecules, and when it does the chemical swells and the strip's resistance to electricity changes. So, by measuring the amount of electricity that passes through each strip, a particular combination of smell-molecules (which make up a particular smell) can be identified. Advanced robot noses like this can tell the difference between spearmint and peppermint.

One of the latest hazard robots is called Urbie. It doesn't have any arms or hands but is very rugged and can clamber up stairs or over rubble using its caterpillar tracks. It's equipped with a laser rangefinder, which is a device that can measure distances very accurately. By sweeping its laser beam all over the place, Urbie can work out a three-dimensional map of whatever mess its owners have got it into. Also, it has a special "omnicam" which means it can see all round at once. So it's very hard to creep up on. It's also very tough – it can easily survive a fall from a second-storey window. And if it falls on its back, it can turn itself over again.

URBIE

TWO EYES FOR 3-D VISION

Urbie is designed to explore hazardous areas devastated by bombs, disasters or even by its colleagues, whom we'll meet in the next chapter...

ROBOT WARS

The image of a war robot is something like the Terminator – highly advanced, unstoppable, deadly, scary glowing eyes, muttering "no problemo" after it's killed someone. But real war robots aren't like this, and perhaps never will be, because it would be incredibly expensive to build such tough machines. It's much easier to make them cheap and cheerful and expect most of them to get "killed". In fact, some war robots are actually designed to destroy themselves – they will be dropped from planes, and when they land, they'll be able to crawl to wherever they'll do most harm before blowing themselves and their targets up.

The idea of a fighting robot goes back many years: humanoid robot soldiers were designed in 1924, and in 1939, visitors to the New York Exhibition were greeted by a half-tonne, 2.8 m, radio-controlled fighting robot. It had arms and legs and was equipped with metal clubs and suffocating gases.

Now, robots that play at war are really popular, and slug it out on TV in programmes such as *Robot Wars*, *Battlebots* and *Robotica*. They're called things like Pretty Hate Machine, Sergeant Bash and the especially deadly Sir Killalot.

Name: Sir Killalot
Function: fighting puppet robot, seen on TV series *Robot Wars*
Date of first appearance: 1998
Special abilities: equipped with spiked lance and pincers operated by an eight-horsepower hydraulic pump
Appearance: armoured and spiky
Weaknesses: can only move at 13 km per hour, so fairly easy to escape from if you're not cornered
Robot-spotters' notes: strong and agile enough to be able to pirouette while holding a robot and then fling them out of the arena

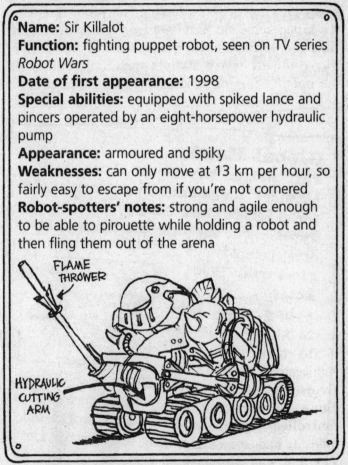

FLAME THROWER

HYDRAULIC CUTTING ARM

In reality, there are two main types of war robots: spies and fighters. Let's begin with cyberspies:

Predator

Type: remote-controlled flying surveillance plane

Length: over 8 m

Wingspan: nearly 15 m

Maximum flying time: over 40 hours

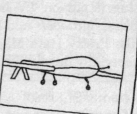

In service since: early 1990s

Note: flew 128 spying missions in the Gulf War

Global Hawk

Full name: The Global Hawk High-Altitude Long-Endurance Unmanned Aerial Vehicle (HAE UAV)

Type: robotic spy-plane (currently under development)

First trial: 1998

Notes:

• uses visual light, radar or infra-red to map over 4,000 square km an hour from a height of up to 20 km

• can spot objects only 30 cm across

• once given its destination, works out the best route, avoiding bad weather and flying in complicated patterns to make it hard to track.

Cypher

Type: circular flying robot with ability to hover. Works in a team of three robots 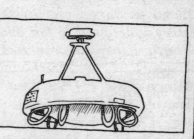 which communicate with each other and their base by radio (whole group is called the Multipurpose Security and Surveillance Mission Platform (MSSMP)).

Size: 1.8 m

First tested: 1997

Equipped with:

• video cameras sensitive to heat as well as light

• laser range finder (distance-measuring device)

• sensitive microphones.

Notes: Cyphers keep the number of radio signals they send to their base as short and infrequent as they can, to give them less chance of being detected and tracked. Programmed to decide for themselves what they think sounds or looks suspicious and to home in and spy on their own before reporting back to base.

Microspies

The big problem with most robotic spies is that they're easy to spot. But soon, there will be spy robots too small to notice, only a few millimetres long and equipped with cameras and microphones.

To speed micro-spy robots up, and to give them better access to what they want to spy on, it makes sense to teach them to fly like their bigger cousins. So, soon there will be robot bugs disguised as bugs. One of these under development at the moment is the micromechanical flying insect (MFI), which is the size of a housefly. A prototype should be ready in 2004. Other types of MAVs (Micro Air Vehicles) fly by using tiny propellers or helicopter blades.

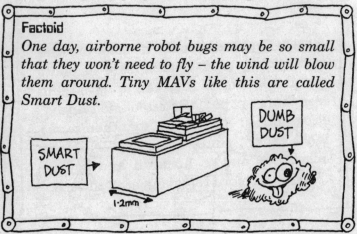

Invisibots

There are lots of ways for war robots to remain undetected. They have some advantages over people anyway – they don't smell like we do and they don't generate heat when they're not doing anything, so guard dogs and heat-detectors can't find them. To make them hard to see, they can be painted with leafy colours like human soldiers' uniforms, or, weirdly enough, they can have bright lights stuck to them. This works especially well when they're positioned on the horizon. They can avoid sticking out like a sore end-effector digit by adjusting the lights until they're exactly as bright as the sky behind them. Some fish do this too, to avoid being seen by predators from below.

And of course, since robots can be made in all shapes and sizes, they can easily be disguised as almost anything...

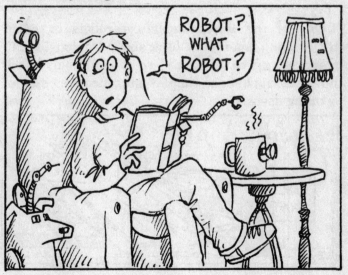

Battlebots

So far, humans haven't really trusted robots enough to equip them with much in the way of weapons. Though bomb-disposal robots are sometimes equipped with shotguns, they're never given any control over them. But a few robots have been given tranquillizer darts, while others have a special sticky foam which can be squirted at people to immobilize them. A trendy new weapon, also for bomb-disposal robots, is a disruptor, which is a suitably techy name for a water-pistol.

One of the latest battlefield robots is called SPIKE, and is a robotic tank about 1 m long. It can travel at up to 25 kph — so it can easily catch humans. It has a simple but effective way of opening doors...

...and can fire exploding shells at people.

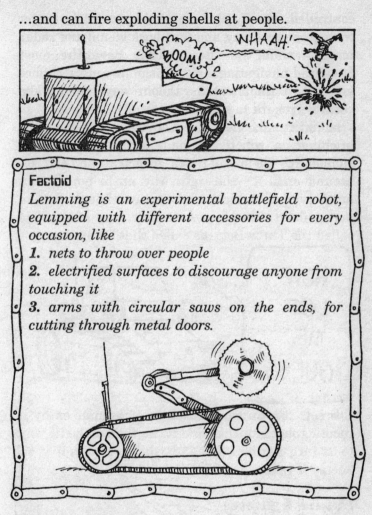

Factoid

Lemming is an experimental battlefield robot, equipped with different accessories for every occasion, like

1. nets to throw over people

2. electrified surfaces to discourage anyone from touching it

3. arms with circular saws on the ends, for cutting through metal doors.

Weapons 'R' us

Some robots aren't just equipped with weapons, that's actually what they are.

Cruise missiles are by far the most deadly war robots in use at present. They are remote-controlled, low-flying bombs able to hit a target with great accuracy, and feed back visual and radar images while they do it. They have the most advanced navigational systems of any mobile robot and fly in complicated random ways that make them very hard to shoot down.

In 2000, another self-destroying warbot was invented, a robotic grenade called the Sandia Hopper. It's the size of a half-grapefruit and can roll around until it's the right way up to hop. It can jump over 6 m high, and carries enough fuel to make about 100 hops. A similar type of robot is called the ThrowBot. It's called that because...

NOW LET ME GUESS...

Correct. It's thrown, either by a human or by a robotic robot launcher, and it can then make its way to its target or blow itself up when it senses that an enemy is near.

Future fighters

There are plenty of reasons to think that there will be lots more war robots in future. Human soldiers, however fierce and loyal, nearly always have to make sure they stay alive. But robots don't, so they can do a lot more dangerous things.

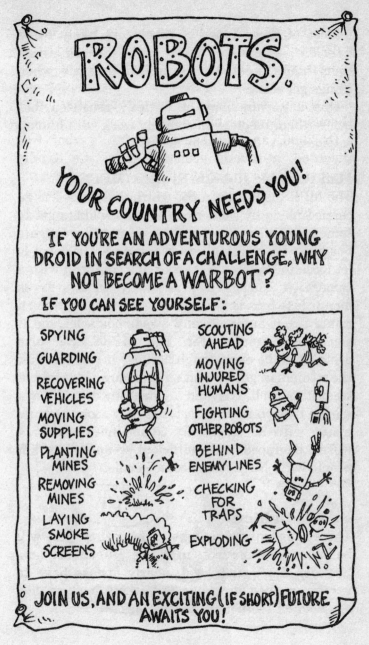

Most of these types of robots are likely to be hybrids – left to their own devices when everything's quiet, but controlled remotely when things get scary.

One day, wars may be entirely robotized, but before then, robots will probably work with human soldiers, just like this one does:

Man Portable Robotic System (MPRS)
The MPRS is a little robot which is designed to be carried along by soldiers. When the soldiers get to somewhere like a sewer they want to investigate but don't fancy going into themselves, the robot is let loose to explore on its own. It's equipped with a camera, it can go just as easily backwards as forwards (which is handy if there's no space to turn round in), it automatically avoids obstacles and it can travel underwater. The MPRS was also designed to be extra tough because it was felt that the soldiers might be a bit on the rough side and not treat it too well. They did accidentally drop it down a huge hole on its first test, but they soon got quite matey with it. Their only complaint was that it wasn't equipped with sufficient weaponry to kill people with. No pleasing some people.

Most of the funding for robotic research comes from the military, which is another reason to think that war robots have a bright future. Bright for them anyway. Whether it's something for humans to look forward to is a lot more dubious. It might be – if in future wars are fought *only* by robots, it will save a lot of human deaths on the battlefield – but who knows what a robot army might be used for once it's won a war? Wiping out human populations would be no problem.

It's easy to make a robotic killer, but it's a lot more difficult to make robots that can cure people. However, they do exist...

CYBERDOCS

There are quite a few fictional cyborgs about – the Borg, Robocop, the Daleks, the Cybermen, and, if you can remember him, Steve Austin, the Six Million Dollar Man.

All these creatures are part human, part machine, and all are extra macho thanks to their mechanical bits. Such machines aren't too far from reality, and their ancestors go back a very long way indeed.

As long ago as 1509, wounded knights were being fitted with mechanical hands which contained ratchets so that the fingers would stay in place once they'd been curled around something. They could be released by flicking a lever. By the 1700s, there were mechanical legs too, one of which made a loud clapping sound when its owner, the Marquis of Anglesey, walked about – which must have made it very tricky for him to creep up on people.

YOU CAN HARDLY TELL THE DIFFERENCE

CRASH! BANG! WOLLOP!

Of course, these machines weren't robots, but they were the start of a long line of devices which could be attached to people to help them when their bodies failed. Over the next few centuries, artificial limbs gradually became lighter, more comfortable and more realistic, but it wasn't until the mid-20th century that powered ones were invented. They used compressed air or electric motors to allow the user to open and close their artificial hands. More recently, powered artificial legs have been developed too.

To begin with, powered artificial limbs were about as strong as human ones, but in 1966 a mechanical body called Hardiman was developed to be more powerful than a human. The user had to climb inside Hardiman, which then reacted to the movements they made by copying them, but with greatly increased force.  Hardiman was intended to be used in warehousing and building, but it went out of control very easily and could give the user and the surroundings a right battering when it did. In any case, conventional robots took over many of the jobs it was designed for.

The trouble with Hardiman was that it reacted to the physical movements of the user inside. Real bodies react to signals we send down our nerves from our brains, and robotic limbs that can do this were developed in the early 1980s. In 1982, a paralysed man was the first to walk with robot legs controlled in this way.

NUTS AND BOLTS: HUMAN/MACHINE LINKAGES

1. Some artificial limbs are moved directly by the remaining muscles of the user. The user wears a harness system to pick up the muscle movements, attached to a cable which transmits the movements from the harness to the limb. Though it takes quite a lot of practice to get used to these limbs, they are light and relatively cheap. Also, the user's muscles can feel any resistance to the limb – so they can judge the weight of an object an artificial arm picks up. These "body-powered" limbs are also tough and can be used in wet or dusty environments.

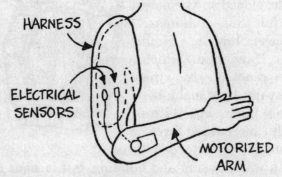

HARNESS

ELECTRICAL SENSORS

MOTORIZED ARM

2. Other artificial limbs contain sensors which are very sensitive to tiny electrical signals. We use signals like these to control our own muscles: the brain sends them down nerves and our muscles flex in response. In the artificial limb, the sensors pick up these signals, and they are used to operate motors. These limbs, though much more difficult to build and still being developed at the moment, will be much easier to use: their owners will eventually be able to move the limbs in just the same way that they move their real ones.

But people don't just move their limbs, they get messages from them too. Whether you're a person or a robot, if your hand doesn't tell you how hard you're squeezing an egg or something, you don't know when to stop applying more pressure.

HOW DO YOU... OOOPS!

Feedback from an artificial hand is much more limited than from a real one, but what can be done is to include a pressure-sensor in the hand (see page 56). The more pressure the sensor measures, the more electricity it produces. The electricity is amplified and fed to what is left of the user's real limb, where it's felt as a tingle like a very mild electric shock. With practice, the user can judge the firmness of the grip from the strength of the tingle.

Robosurgeons

Because they move so precisely and their end effectors are so steady, robots are better at some surgical operations than people. NeuroMate has carried out well over 2,000 brain operations, and Robodoc has helped with over 5,000 hip replacements.

151

Robodoc at work

Before surgery, the patient has three pins inserted into their leg bone, and then has a series of X-rays taken from different angles.

A computer transforms these X-rays into a 3-D map of the leg bone, with the positions of the pins marked.

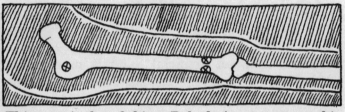

This map is then fed into Robodoc's computer and is also used by the human surgeons to work out exactly the shape that needs to be cut out of the bone.

The patient's leg is fixed in place and Robodoc is wheeled up to it and locked in position. It detects the exact locations of the three pins, and uses the 3-D map to work out exactly where it needs to cut.

Then a special drill is connected to Robodoc's manipulator and it drills out the shape the surgeons instruct it to. Human surgeons then take over and insert the hip replacement.

Robotic surgeons are very handy, but they still need a human to slice open a person for them before they can operate – which often takes longer to recover from than the operation itself. But...

Factoid

A hybrid robot called Cleo is being developed to investigate illnesses and it fits inside the human intestine. It's about 3 cm long, has sensors that can detect light and heat, feelers to locate obstacles, caterpillar tracks and a claw, and can be steered round inside people by a doctor with a joystick. One day, Cleo might be used to cut away diseased tissue, before sucking it away through a tube.

SAUSAGE? YUK!

Cleo's much too big to get inside other parts of people, like their veins, but one day, even smaller robots might be small enough to actually enter people's bodies through a hypodermic syringe. They might even be too small to see...

Nanobots

A hundred years ago, a lot of scientists didn't believe that atoms or molecules – the tiny particles from which all substances are made – really existed. Now they are able to move individual ones around and stick them together. They've even made little stick people out of them. Very clever, you're probably thinking, but what's the point? Well, what if the stick people could walk? Robots like this are really being investigated, though they look more like little sets of cogs and wheels than people. They're called nanobots, because they're a few nanometres in size (a nanometre is a thousandth of a millionth of a metre – which means a teaspoon could hold several thousand million nanobots).

To make a nanobot you need to stick lots of atoms together, which would be easy if they weren't about a ten-millionth of a millimetre across.

An instrument called a scanning tunnelling microscope (STM), with an incredibly sharp tip, is used both to "see" the atoms and to pick them up and move them around. The atoms are stuck to other atoms to build up whatever shape is wanted. In 1990, IBM scientists arranged 35 atoms into the letters IBM using an STM, and since then they've built both electronic parts like wires and transistors and mechanical ones like levers and gears. From there, they will move on to build nanofactory machines, which will be able to mass produce nanobots.

NANOBOT

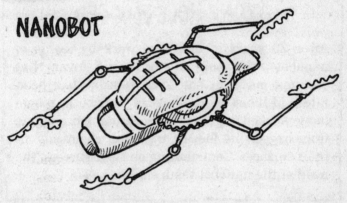

Nanobots could be equipped with little spikes and knives, and be used to clear cholesterol layers from inside arteries, the tubes through which blood flows from the heart and through our bodies. (It's these layers which you get from eating too many chips and doughnuts. When the artery is too narrow, too little blood can pass through it, and you can suffer a heart attack.) After they've done their bit, the nanobots could stay around to check on the level of cholesterol or sugar in the blood. These nanobots will need to be coated with something which the human body won't react to, like diamond. They will probably use ultrasound to communicate with people and each other, since this travels well through soggy things like bodies.

And nanobots may not be restricted just to medical work...

ROBOT'S REALM

INCORPORATING AUTOMATIC LAWNMOWER MONTHLY

OZONE HOLE PLUGGED

After 20 years of intensive work by teams of nanobots, the hole in the ozone layer that humans made in the 20th century has been filled. Millions of millions of nanobotic robots have worked together, generating more ozone from oxygen in the air by using chemicals on their surfaces. Commenting on their success, the head of the nanobot team said, "No problem."

ATTACK OF THE ACRONYMS

Whether you want to be a robotocist, or just understand what they're on about, you'll have to get into acronyms: WIWTCIA*.

Try sorting out what stands for what in our quick quiz and then when you've finished, count up all your correct answers and find out how cybernetically clever or droidfully dumb you really are...

1. AERCAM
a) Android ElectRonic Construction And Maintenance
b) Autonomous Extravehicular activity Robotic CAMera
c) Automatic Earth-Return and Communication Astronautical Mission

2. AI
a) Articulated Insectoid
b) Artificial Intelligence
c) Automaton Insurance

3. AUV
a) Autonomous Underwater Vehicle
b) Asonically Understood Vocalization
c) Anti-Unimate Verdict

4. CURV
a) Cybernetic Underwater Robotic Vessel
b) Calibrated Universal Radar Vision
c) Cable-controlled Undersea Recovery Vehicle

*Which Is What This Chapter Is About

157

5. GPS

a) Global Positioning System

b) Geo-Physical Scanner

c) General-Purpose Software

6. HAE UAV

a) Holistic Automatic Environment for Underwater Android Validation

b) Hazard And Emergency conditions Under Automatic Vision control

c) High-Altitude long-Endurance Unmanned Aerial Vehicle

7. MAV

a) Micro Air Vehicle

b) Machine-Assisted Verbalization

c) Mechanically-Adapted Voice

8. MFI

a) Marine Flow Investigator

b) Mechanical Friends Incorporated

c) Micromechanical Flying Insect

9. MPRS

a) Man-Portable Robotic System

b) Microwave-Proton-Radiation Scanner

c) Microbotic Programmable Retrieval System

10. MSSMP
a) Machine-Selected Space Mission Profile
b) Multipurpose Security and Surveillance Mission Platform
c) Meteorological Survey and Storm Modelling Program

11. PUMA
a) Precision Underwater Mechanical Android
b) Programmable Ultrasonic Manufacturing Automaton
c) Programmable Universal Machine for Assembly

12. ROV
a) Randomly Organised Version
b) Remotely Operated Vehicle
c) Robot-Organic Variant

13. RMS
a) Remote Manipulator System
b) Robotic Mission Statement
c) Random Memory Search

14. SCARA
a) Selective Compliance Assembly Robot Arm
b) SCan-And-Retrieve Android
c) SCience And Research Automaton

15. STM
a) Sensory Translation Machine
b) Stress-Tensioned Mechanism
c) Scanning Tunnelling Microscope

How did you do?

0 – 3 correct   Major re-programming of expert system required.

4 – 7 correct   A few programs short of a neural net yet.

8 – 11 correct   Just one or two screws loose here and there.

12 – 15 correct   Intelligence unit capable of fully autonomous operation.

If you got more than three correct, you're ready for the next chapter. If you're feeling brave that is...

RIOTOUS ROBOTS?

The robots we've talked about in this book aren't exactly riotous – the few that have killed people were only obeying their instructions, not rioting because of lack of oil or because they were sick of hoovering or anything.

But are robots really dangerous?

At the moment, robots don't have minds of their own so they couldn't "deliberately" kill anyone. But factory robots have accidentally killed several people who were trying to repair them with the power still switched on, and as long ago as 1932, at the Chicago World's Fair, a robot is supposed to have killed its maker with an iron club – the police concluded that someone must have programmed the robot to do it, but the human murderer was never found.

Though not the sort of thing that happens too often at the moment, this use of robots as murder weapons could increase as the number of robots controlled by radio-links increases. Hackers who are clever enough to get into top secret bank and government files and mess about with them wouldn't have too much difficulty breaking into coded signals too. They could replace them with their own instructions and make the robots do whatever they liked, even from thousands of kilometres away. It would be almost impossible to trace the hacker, so it could be the perfect crime.

But robots can be deadly even if no one orders them to be, because:

- though in many ways they're brilliant, in others they're a bit stupid: certainly not clever enough to know that they might hurt a person who gets in their way
- they're strong, often much stronger than humans
- they can move their limbs very fast indeed
- they suddenly burst into activity when they react to something, unlike human workers who nearly always fold their newspapers, put down their cups of tea and grumble first.

In factories, there's quite a bit that can be done to cope with dangerous robots: they're kept in cages, given sensors to detect people, fitted with warning lights and buzzers and surrounded with STOP buttons. (Though these aren't much good for coping with modern super-fast robots that can slice your head off before you can say, "Goodness, that looks terribly sharp."*)

And the people who work with factory robots are given dull training courses to learn how to treat

*If you've ever seen the classic 1951 robot film *The Day the Earth Stood Still*, you'll know that to stop a robot what you really have to say is "Klaatu: borada. Nikto."

them: not to approach them when they're working, keep the door of their cage locked and use the nearest STOP button at the first sign of danger.

But none of these techniques is much good outside a factory.

Revolting robots

According to some people, robots may soon get a lot more dangerous. They say that humans are in charge of the Earth only because they're the most intelligent things around. But robot intelligence is developing much faster than human intelligence is – robot brains have developed more in the last 50 years than human brains have in the last 50 million (in fact, some roboticists estimate that robot intelligence is increasing ten million times faster than ours!). So one day soon – almost certainly in your lifetime – robots will become cleverer than people, so *they* will be the most intelligent things around, at which point they'll naturally take charge of the Earth. Given the brilliant way robots communicate with each other, even a single intelligent robot could do it, just by overriding the human control of its dumber colleagues and telling them to rebel. Even now, computers and robots help to design and build each other and they'll soon be in control of robot-making factories, so riotous robots could reproduce very rapidly, before people even knew what was happening.

The idea that the robots of the future might be dangerous isn't confined to science fiction. Many roboticists, like Kevin Warwick, take it very seriously. Of course, there are plenty of objections to the idea of riotous robots – but there are also plenty of answers to the objections. Have a look at some of the main ones and make your own mind up:

A robot can never be cleverer than the person who designs it.

So how can a chess robot defeat humans?

We could always just stop improving robotic intelligence.

But without more intelligence, robots won't get any more useful than they are already. And there's a lot of money to be made from more useful robots.

Robots can never really think, however cleverly they behave.

How could we ever know whether or not a robot is thinking? Anyway, to riot, all a robot needs to do is make a decision, whether they think it over in the way we do or not, and they do that all the time already.

Robots need never be given the chance to take charge.

But robots were invented to take over from us: there's no point in having a security robot that can't make decisions, even if there are some things it might decide that you may not agree with. And if there are two armies of war robots, one making its own decisions and the other constantly referring to humans, the self-controlled ones would be a lot faster.

Wouldn't a robot just use its intelligence to work out that it's wrong to kill people?

Robots might notice that they're expendable and would treat humans in the same way. Or perhaps they'd work out that "killing" robots is wrong too, and take action to make sure humans couldn't do it.

Why not just program robots not to hurt people, like Asimov said?

If a robot is a lot cleverer than a person it might find a way round any instruction it was given. It might reason that "don't hurt people" meant it was still allowed to order another robot to hurt people, even though it couldn't do the job itself. Or it might decide to kill people without hurting them, or it might work out that it was OK to hurt a single person, so long as it didn't hurt several "people".

OK, OK, then just switch them off!

It's not always that easy: a clever robot could soon find a way to protect itself. And robots won't always be so dependent on electrical power supplies: as we've seen already, they can live on slugs – and alcohol would also be a good source of energy. (Which is why Bender likes a scotch or two.)

We'll have to be very sure that we do want robots to do what we tell them. There is a story called With Folded Hands* in which life becomes a nightmare because robots have been told not to allow any harm to come to humans. To do this, the robots don't allow people to do anything whatsoever, just in case they hurt themselves. So the humans just have to sit there – with folded hands.

CRAZY!

*By Jack Williamson, 1947.

Robots of tomorrow

Whether they're dangerous or not, what will the robots of the future be like? At the moment, a robot's body only makes it good at a certain range of tasks. But scientists are working on robots than can change shape. These will be very useful in space or when rescuing people, where conditions are hard to predict but getting a second robot on the scene would be too difficult or take too long.

NUTS AND BOLTS: SHAPECHANGERS

1. In the same way that robots can already learn how to do things by a trial-and-error approach applied to their programs, these shape-shifters can try out different physical forms to see how well they work. They could make their new bits on something called a 3-D printer which uses a jet of quick-setting plastic to make different shapes. The first experiments with these robots involved giving them tasks like "learn to move". A group of them came up with all sorts of different solutions, like pushing themselves along with one leg, squirming like maggots or scuttling sideways like crabs.

2. A modular or fractal robot is made of tiny interlocking robotic building blocks which link themselves together like Lego. One use for this type of robot is to build itself into walls around hazardous things like damaged nuclear reactors. And if a part of such a robot were damaged, it could simply replace itself with more robot blocks. Or it could pass through small openings by taking itself apart, going through bit by bit and reassembling itself afterwards.

Mind control

We might control robots of the future with our thoughts. Thoughts generate electrical impulses*, and there's no reason why these impulses couldn't be used to send radio messages to control robots. This has been done successfully with a rat, who learned to operate a water-dropper by its brain power, and, in 2000, with a monkey. The monkey's mind was linked to a robot arm, so that whenever the monkey moved its real arm, the robot arm moved too – even though it was 90 km away at the time. In 2001, a "mind-switch" was demonstrated in London, which switched on a light when people closed their eyes. It was operated by the natural changes in brainwaves that occur when we shut

*Some people say that thoughts *are* electrical impulses.

our eyes. A special machine called an electroencephalograph picked up the brainwaves through sensitive electrical detectors on the scalp. A computer then analysed the shapes of the waves. When the waves had the distinctive shapes that form when we close our eyes, the computer sent a signal to a light bulb to switch it on.

The robofuture

Roboticists like nothing better than predicting the future of robots (apart from actually building them, that is), and most agree that the key to robotic development is advances in AI: as soon as a robot can be made clever enough to do a job, it will be a doddle to give it the body it needs. So, working on the likely rate of improvement of AI systems, some roboticists reckon the robofuture *might* look a little bit like this...

2010s Robots are as brainy as tortoises – able to feed and look after themselves most of the time in the environments they're designed for – like farms or gardens or beaches. They can avoid really obvious dangers like fire, but aren't able to cope with dangers they're not programmed about – like cars. Their hands are advanced enough to pick up delicate objects, but still too clumsy to do anything fiddly like thread a needle.

They can communicate with humans by artificial speech and recognize simple one-word responses, though they can't chat. They are good at simple security and cleaning jobs, but can't cope for too long without human assistance.

2020s Robots are as clever as rats, which means they can survive in lots of environments, even ones they're not really expecting (so a beachbot could cope with a supermarket). They are able to learn rapidly, though people will still need to give them quite a bit of help: a robot like this would be able to locate and pull up plants from the garden, but its owner would need to spend a lot of time showing it which were weeds. They can carry on simple conversations with people, and can be left to get on with their jobs without needing a human to keep an eye on them, though they are likely to need to ask for help from time to time.

2030s Robots are as clever as monkeys, able to survive

and work in almost any environment, even dangerous ones like swamps or building sites. They need a lot less help from people. They are able to work out their own ways of solving problems, so once a person has given them an instruction like "clear the table but leave the candles" they can check online libraries to find out what a candle looks like, rather than needing to ask (as a 2020s robot would have to). By now, because they have the intelligence to use them, their hands are almost as adaptable as ours, but much stronger. Though they still can't chat, they can understand complicated verbal instructions.

2040s Robots can do all the jobs that people want them to. They are as clever as human beings, with the ability to reason. In some ways, they're as good as people. In others, they're better. Which means that, around 2050, they ... well, you'll just have to wait and see...

Robots 'R' us?

Even if people find a way to keep robots under control, there are many questions still to be answered:

- As robots become more advanced, they will become more similar to us, until they are like slaves: intelligent creatures being forced to do boring jobs for nothing in return. By then, people will have robotic friends, just like they have robotic pets now. Will people be happy that robots like their friends are slaves?

- Will robots become so like us that they start to demand rights for themselves? How could you argue against them – don't we have more rights than animals because we're more intelligent?
- And then what happens when robots become more intelligent than us? Will they demand *more* rights than humans have, just as we have more rights than animals? What could that mean?
- The difference between people and robots is bound to decrease as robots become more human. But, while this is happening, we're bound to become more robotic ourselves, as sophisticated implants are developed to help weak hearts, brittle bones, damaged ears and teeth. We're used to very simple implants

already, like pacemakers, pins in broken bones and false teeth, but it's not likely to stop with cleverer versions of these. What about plastic implants for stronger muscles? Internal devices that clean and feed our blood? Or even brain implants that give us better memories, faster mathematical skills, more control over our emotions? With computerized brains and robotized bodies, will humans become robots?

The world of the future will be a world of robots. And those robots might be us.

UPDATE YOUR CHIPS

We're living in an exciting time for robots: they're developing more rapidly than ever and in the next few years we're going to see a lot more of them. These websites will keep you informed about bot's going on:

- **Cool Robot of the Week site:**
http://ranier.hq.nasa.gov/telerobotics_page/coolrobots.html
- **Reading University cyborg research site:**
http://www.cyber.rdg.ac.uk
- **Androids:**
http://www.androidworld.com
- **Humanoid robots:**
http://www.ai.mit.edu/projects/humanoid-robotics-group
- **Talk to a computer program called ELIZA on:**
http://www.manifestation.com/neurotoys/eliza.php3
- **Other "chatterbot" sites:**
http://www.alicebot.org
http://www.maybot.com
- **Another robot site:**
http://www.bbc.co.uk/science/robots
- **Info about Cog:**
http://caes.mit.edu/mvp/html/cog.html
- **UK robot wars sites:**
http://www.tectonic.force9.co.uk; www.robotwars.co.uk
- **US robot wars sites:**
http://www.battlebots.com; www.robotmayhem.com

A few years ago, you needed lots of money to build your own robot. Now you can make some amazing robots yourself without needing a lot of cash. Books like these will show you how. They're listed in order of difficulty, the first in the list contains the easiest projects and the last, the most difficult.

- *How to Build a Robot*, Clive Gifford, Oxford University Press, 2000 (this one doesn't actually tell you how to build a robot, but it does include several simple experiments in robotics)
- *The Robot Builder's Bonanza*, Gordon McComb, McGraw-Hill, 2000
- *Robots, Androids and Animatrons: 12 Incredible Projects You Can Build*, John Iovine, McGraw-Hill, 2001 (2nd edition)
- *Build Your Own Combat Robot*, Pete Miles and Tom Carroll, Osborne, 2002
- *Mobile Robots*, Joe Jones and Anita Flynn, 1999
- *Build Your Own Robot*, Karl Lunt, AK Peters, 2000